We are like books. Most people only see our cover, the minority read only the introduction, many people believe the critics. Few will know our content.

Émile Zola

Christopher 'Gyp' Davies

A Valleys Legend

Mike Church

y Lolfa

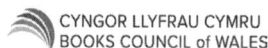

Llywodraeth Cymru
Welsh Government

Cymru Greaðigol
Creative Wales

CYNGOR LLYFRAU CYMRU
BOOKS COUNCIL of WALES

First impression: 2024

The publishers wish to acknowledge the support
of the Books Council of Wales and Creative Wales.

Cover design: Sion Ilar

ISBN: 978-1-80099-597-0

Published and printed in Wales
on paper from well-maintained forests by
Y Lolfa Cyf., Talybont, Ceredigion SY24 5HE
website www.ylolfa.com
e-mail ylolfa@ylolfa.com
tel 01970 832 304

Contents

Voices from Underground 7

Foreword 11

A Vote of Thanks 15

What they're saying about this book 16

A note from the author 19

Not another book about miners... 21

In the beginning 26

What's in a name? 29

Roots 36

A union man 43

Mining 48

Women 69

Like father like son and the dreaded drink 85

A sporting life 107

The day Gyp met The King 117

Mental health and well-being 126

Getting to know you 136

Caerau Men's Shed 142

Life Beyond the Shed Door 147

Politician 152

Epilogue 154

Appendix: *Life Beyond the Shed Door* 159

Voices from Underground

You can still hear those voices from underground boys,
Although the tools have been put on the bar
For the last time,
The mandrill, sledge, hatchet and banjo

Those voices
Listen to them
They are the voices
Of the brave colliers of the past
Who hewed that first lump of coal
Out of the guts of the earth
Hauntingly calling to you
They will never go away

Stand still boys in the empty void
And listen to the echoes of the past
As they come flooding like waves
To fill your senses
Sometimes suffocating
Like the black dust
That we choked on

It's here
You can sense it
You can taste it
Coal
It's in your blood
It courses through your veins
You'll never escape it
It consumes you

Voices from underground
That only a miner would understand
'Fire in the hole!'
Up goes the shout
As we blasted away
The ground shaking under your feet
The fall of rock
Wooden posts cracking under the weight

Men groaning in pain
Sinews straining
Sweat dripping off the end of your nose
A reminder of the days
Grafting at the coal face
That stale hot air
Black dust swirling
Filling your nostrils and lungs
As you dig your way to heaven boys

Then like a dream it's all gone
Years of that life below ground
Yes there will be legends
But at what cost?

Empty are the coal faces
'One last push forward boys!'
The distant disappearing cry

Gone are the headings of hard rock
The fish plates, the steel rings and the timber

Empty are the conveyors
That carried the coal to the dump
Feeding that ever hungry mouth

Gone are the drams
Bursting with coal
Records broken each back-breaking shift

Empty are the cages
Packed with colliers
Like sardines in a tin
Descending to the pit bottom

Empty are the pit head baths
Once so full of steam, laughter and song

Gone are the locker rooms
Full of black dusty clothes
Where we used to sit and smoke Woodbines
And talk of shifts gone by

A generation lost
Amongst the chaos
With empty hopes
And broken hearts

And empty too
Are the hearts that closed the pits
And caused the death of mining
The death of communities by their hundreds
Still they struggle
Gone are their dreams
Their futures
Families clinging to what's left

So is there hope left in our valley?

We shall not bend like reeds in the wind
We have fought these battles before
Time and time again
Shoulder to shoulder

'It's yours if you want it'
Whisper the voices from underground.

Christopher 'Gyp' Davies

Foreword

by Roy Noble MBE

At LONG LAST I've read your book… the story of a miner, Mike. I thought it was excellent and with so much I could relate to. The 'accolades' given to you by established writers such as Catrin Collier, Phil Carradice and others really underlined your research and subsequent storytelling.

Characters like Gyp were to be found in my village, Brynaman, and the nearby mining village of GCG (Gwaun-Cae-Gurwen).

Dai the Gate was one, or Dai Gât, so-called because he'd once lived in the small tollgate. It was one-and-a-bit bedrooms for a family of eight children, I believe. Dai never 'officially' held certain jobs but he was the one called on for digging graves and throwing in any ton of concessionary coal for the widows. He was also a double figures man on pints of beer… double figures before tea-time!

I have met quite a few men, notably in the Dulais Valley, who were a thorn in the management's side in negotiation or disputes during the 1984 strike in particular.

I can recall two union men managed to get the bank manager in Neath to give them all the NUM's local money, for hiding and safe-keeping, because Maggie Thatcher was after it. They carried thousands of pounds around Neath in two plastic Tesco bags.

I loved the way Gyp got his name and his positive association with Travellers. They were common in my area too, selling pegs and cleaning cloths in particular – although we were told by our parents that we were not to play near 'Mynydd llusi' (Whinberry Mountain), because the 'gyps' lived there and we could be kidnapped.

I remember the day my grandfather got killed and they brought his body home. I was only seven at the time but it is still clear in my mind, as is the day they brought my father home from working underground because a large service pipe had blown up in his face.

I could relate to Gyp's rugby days too.

Brynaman was a dangerous place to be on a Saturday if Brynaman RFC were playing away and they were short of players. If you were walking down the road, on a message for your mother, a twenty-eight seater Bedford bus would quietly ease up behind you and you were kidnapped off the road... and your mother didn't know where the hell you were! On one occasion I ended up playing, in thrown-together kit, as a right winger whilst the bus driver was playing on the left wing... in brogues!

I can remember the pit ponies racing around a field on their holiday fortnight off. I remember the Miners' Institutes, the fights in bars, the dances on Saturday nights and the scuffles over girls.

You always made sure, if you were lucky enough to pick up a girl in the dance a quarter of an hour before the buses went, that she was going up the same valley as yourself. You also had to gauge whether it would be worth getting off the bus with the girl if she was living lower down the valley than you. We, as a gang, once asked a known rake, Edwin Davies, if he'd ever struck lucky... and he replied, 'Only twice boys, only twice... but it was worth it.'

The signs and the ethos of mining and miners are still within the fabric of the Valleys. These tribal members of the Welsh Klondike are the melting pot that made up the valleys. They are still there in the souls of the various Valleys... with their contributions to the institutes and structure of each village, they brought culture, education, politics, entertainment, bands, choirs, colourful carnivals, writers and international players of sport.

I recently attended Tyrone O'Sullivan's funeral, he of the famed Tower Colliery buy-out in the Thatcher days.

I am also proud to be the patron of the Aber Valley Heritage Group, who look after the Senghenydd Colliery Disaster Memorial Site and Centre. I attended there recently too, to help them with some visitors at the site. They are an extraordinary group and here's a scandal – soon after the second disaster at Senghenydd, in 1913, charity contributions reached a total of what would now be £12 million pounds... and that money has disappeared. Three banks cannot trace it apparently, even though they have been pressurised by elected members. My word, that heritage group and that community could do with that money right now.

Your book brought back such recall in my life, as it would in the lives of everyone brought up in the mining communities. A job well done in capturing the memory of one leading actor in the passing drama of the years.

Congratulations on a really great book,

Roy

A Vote of Thanks

THIS BOOK HAS been written with the cooperation and help of many people and so it is right to give them a mention and a vote of thanks. Both Gyp and myself have agreed that any profits from the book will go to men's mental health via the Caerau Men's Shed and also Afan and Llynfi Valley Miners.

So, thank you for buying this book. We hope you enjoy it and your money will contribute in some small way, to help in the fight against men suffering social isolation and loneliness.

We dedicate this book to all those miners and their families who lost loved ones through the disasters and hard labour of mining. Those voices from underground will never be forgotten or silenced.

We want to particularly thank the communities of Nantyffyllon and Caerau, many of whom have now had their say in these pages. A special thanks to Gyp's family and friends for all their help putting this book together.

Photographs have been provided by Phil 'the flash' Davies, Verdun Price and Doug Hicks, RCT Libraries, Afan Argoed Mining Museum, and the National Museum of Wales (Ceri Thompson!). Thanks also to Wendy Donovan, Andre Van Wyk and Awen Cultural Trust. We have tried to ensure we have sourced and gained permissions for all the photographs correctly, if any have slipped through the net we wholeheartedly apologise – we did try!

What they're saying about this book

This book has been written as part of a larger project entitled 'Voices from Underground'. The aim was to collect the memories of miners who are rapidly becoming a dying breed. This tale tells the story of one such miner but is dedicated to all those who lost their lives in the hard labour of working underground. As noted, any profits from the sale of this book will go to Caerau Men's Shed and their efforts to get men talking and improve their mental health.

This book isn't just about one man's life, it also tells the real story of life in the Welsh Valleys. It is about the heartaches, the hardships and the sheer glory of never giving up, of being part of a unique community. It's a book that should be in every home in the country.
Phil Carradice, BBC Broadcaster/Historian

I've never met 'Gyp' but after reading Mike's biography of the larger-than-life man, I know him. He epitomises everything that is fine, strong, true and generous in the Welsh (along with a little that is downright naughty, possibly even illegal, but never vicious). I recognise elements of Gyp in my father and the people I grew up with in Pontypridd. After leaving college I worked at Cymer Afan Comprehensive and came to love the plain-spoken (occasionally to the point of bluntness – 'Well, as I see it', hands-on-hips) ways of the people who live in Caerau, Maesteg, Glyncorrwg, Abergwynfi and Blaengwynfi.

Community spirit is alive, well, preserved and lives on, and long may it, in the Welsh Valleys, be warm, all-enveloping, offering a cushion against hardship, a helping hand when most needed, and reassurance that no one is ever alone. Mike Church has conjured the man who was a miner from blank pages, allowing him to step forth into our lives, just as he has created a record of the closing of the south Wales pit and the dying days of the coal industry which has left scars in valleys that have yet to heal – that's if they ever will.

Everyone who has a Gyp in their life is truly blessed. I only hope that men of his ilk survive to guide Wales into the future. A fascinating read, and a great piece of work.

Catrin Collier, bestselling novelist

Miners are an iconic part of Britain's – especially Wales' – industrial and social heritage. A great deal has been written and said about them, but almost always as a group. In a highly readable account, author Mike Church has set out to put that right by focusing on one larger-than-life individual, Christopher 'Gyp' Davies. This is not a formulaic biography but a collection of stories, narratives, interviews, impressions and anecdotes, including reminiscences of Gyp's friends.

As well as making the book easy to digest, it enables Church to present a multi-dimensional account of an extraordinary man in a very manageable format. If you want to make friends with an extraordinary giant, in more senses than one, with an existing piece of our social history, then Mike Church's enjoyable account makes this possible.

Chris Read, Emeritus Professor
of European History, University of Warwick

Really enjoyed. You succeed in bringing Gyp to life completely, we feel like we know him... but then maybe we do. Bits of him remind you of so many people – family and friends – who have been an influence. Gyp's 'ordinary life' is one that really does need to be told. Clearly a man of substance, action and heart, but searingly honest about his flaws too, it is this honesty that gives the book its strength. From the explanation of his – now difficult – nickname to his recollections of his dark, selfish drinking days.

It's completely authentic and will resonate with anyone who has faced struggles at any point in their lives. It is an honest story of a tough rugby man who understands the meaning of true Welsh community spirit. A great read.

James Hook/Dave Brayley, authors of the
***Chasing a Rugby Dream* books**

Christopher Davies is well known to the South Wales Miners' Museum as the one and only Gyp. He is a fantastic character and a keen supporter of the museum. This book gives a great insight into the coal mining industry. It recounts his experiences, knowledge and memories straight from the heart and with coal in his blood. Gyp and his book are both national treasures from deep within the Llynfi Valley.

Charlene Rodger, Manager of
South Wales Mining Museum, Afan Argoed

A note from the author

I WORKED FOR many years as a teacher before giving up the profession to try my luck as a writer and work hands-on in the community. I've been doing that for the last fifteen years, heavily involved in working with schools, residential homes, prisons, libraries and various community groups. It has been an absolute pleasure.

I first met Christopher Davies, Gyp as he's known (more on that nickname in a minute), six years ago when I was asked to capture some stories from the wonderful Caerau Men's Shed. My first meeting with Gyp was like being hit by a tsunami of generosity and warmth; while I was aware that he was also sizing me up to see if I was half-decent enough to be let loose on his wild bunch of ex-miners and subversives.

He stayed in the background and worked hard to ensure everyone else got a chance to say their piece. Now, six years later, we've produced a book that solely tells his story and what a real treasure trove of tales he has to tell.

During those years we've been thrown together a few times, including putting on a drama performance of *The Full Ponty* at the Senedd (the Welsh Assembly), that I was asked to 'help out' with.

We've also chatted together live onstage at a music festival discussing the life and times of Welsh miners and, as a further nod to those colliers, we visited the Big

L–R: Gyp, Mike Church, Charlene Rodger, Roy Meredith and Chris Davies filming the *Voices from Underground – A Dying Breed* documentary for Awen Cultural Trust, 2022 (available to watch on YouTube).

Pit together as part of a documentary film about mining in Wales. There is evidence of that visit and proof that we really have been underground together.

Researching this book has been a life-changer for me and I owe Gyp and his community a huge debt of gratitude for their humour, honesty and their compelling stories.

When we had created a draft copy, containing the photos and the text, I sent it to Gyp and was decidedly nervous waiting to see if he felt it really captured the essence of his story.

I had a reply back a few hours later that simply said: 'Fucking awesome, butty, Gyp xxx. You're a legend butty; if anyone was going to tell my story it was you, butty.'

I'm under no illusions about who the real legend is here...

Not another book about miners…

WHEN I WAS asked to write this book, I was unsure what I might find as I dug deeper into the life of ex-miner Christopher 'Gyp' Davies.

As it turns out the experience has educated me, delighted me, shocked and surprised me. It has left me ,in no uncertain terms, knowing about the hardships and bravery on show by everyone associated with the coal mines of south Wales.

My grandfather was a miner but I grew up in Hertfordshire, which was a cosy, semi-detached life a million miles away from the Valleys of south Wales. My parents, after Second World War service, had bought into the aspirational, giddy heights of grammar schools and suburbia, which was a far cry from their working-class roots.

I have lived in Wales for forty years but still get asked where I'm from with my outsider's accent. Those issues of identity, belonging and togetherness recur throughout this story. The issue of travelling and migration is very pertinent to our tale too.

An awful lot has been written and documented about the pits, but I think Gyp's story is unique and offers a viewpoint rarely heard. Where else could you read about

a fifteen-year-old miner catching live rats with a Mars bar in the horses' stables, and selling them to the older colliers who owned Jack Russells?

Who else has ever eaten vinegar or toothpaste sandwiches?

He is an extraordinary man, as many people in his valley are more than willing to testify as they give their insights into the real Mr Davies. Their comments on the man will pop up throughout the book. These are the people who knew him way back when, and who know him now.

He has had near-death experiences, brushes with the law, depression, extremes of hardship and has come out on the other side. He now looks to the future, absolutely dedicated to his community.

More than anything, I have got to know the real Gyp over the last year writing this, and he is the most honest, generous, tough, kind, sensitive, thoughtful, no-nonsense bloke that I've ever met... without any doubt at all.

The last remaining miners aren't getting any younger and their memories will soon be consigned to places like Big Pit, Rhondda Heritage Park and the South Wales Mining Museum. Here's one miner's story that deserved to be captured and celebrated, lest we ever forget.

You can keep your biographies of twenty-three-year-old Formula One drivers, or morally questionable ex-Prime Ministers. You can keep those entrepreneurs with so much money they can book their own private rocket to space... give me Gyp's story over theirs anytime.

Well, let's start the story and then you can decide.

You don't meet many people better than Gyp. He's always interested in everyone and always looking to improve children's lives. He's done so much to help in the local schools. We're great pals and we've always looked out for each other. Anything anybody wants, he'll do it or he'll get someone else who can. He'll have you in tears because that's the man he is. He's liked by literally everyone in the valley.
Gareth John @Caerau Men's Shed

Well, even though Gyp is a year younger than me, he has been like a dad to me. He's that fatherly figure I never had when I was growing up. He is a man of steel and often used to clobber people in his rugby days, but these days he's replaced it with a good old-fashioned cwtch.

He is the kindest, most supportive person you could ever wish to meet. The man is a giant and not just in stature, he has a big heart too. Gyp is always looking for ways to serve his local community.

They broke the mould when Gyp was created.

Martin Biginelli @Caerau Men's Shed

Gyp and I have been more like family than friends since we were too short to see over Ma Llewellyn's shop counter, well I was too short even if he wasn't! We spent many a happy hour with his mother and father, Doris and Danny, from being young tearaways to being not-so-young tearaways. Doris and Danny were always proud of his achievements. There were many, including on the rugby pitch and basketball court, as well as bringing the management at British Tissues in line while he was the union representative at the Maesteg Paper Mill.

However, his recent selfless dedication to helping others through the Men's Shed, various committees in Caerau and being a local councillor, would have put a massive smile of pride on his parents' faces, as I am sure it does now to his big sister June and brother-in-law Tyrone, along with his friends, of which there are so many. So what about a couple of stories that it is safe to include in this book?

Well Gyp has always been kind and thoughtful, like the time he hung me over the cliff at the old field in Nanty by one leg, but made sure my shoes never fell off. Or the time we were playing on top of Dyffryn Row on a Sunday. It was dinner time and he said to me, 'Don't go home you big baby! Stay out!' Just then his father turned up and shouted, 'Christopher, get home now, you're late for your dinner!' and off he went without a murmur whilst I went home for a right old ear-bashing.

I remember him buying a green Mini when he turned seventeen. He thought he could drive without any lessons, so we took the car to an off-road location for a spin. The day started well and his driving was good but then, as he became more confident, his driving was chaotic and the car ended up being written off in a ditch. I am not sure what happened to that green Mini but the 'Gyp' gave up driving for life!

As we've got older we've remained young at heart and never fail to laugh every two or three sentences when we meet up and reminisce. It's been a pleasure to contribute to a story that covers the life of Gyp, a true family man, a man who has a strong passion for helping others, a man that knows how to have fun, and a man that I am so proud to call my friend.

Dai Treharne, lifelong friend

In the beginning

THIS IS THE story of one man's life in Wales.

He is a local legend in his own lifetime, or maybe he's just an ordinary bloke who captures the spirit of the last sixty-plus years of Welsh history in the south-east corner of the nation.

More particularly, the corner of our nation we want to take you to is the Llynfi Valley and, even more specifically, we'll go to a little-known village called Nantyffyllon.

This is a story that straddles the golden age of Welsh industrial heritage and brings us to the post-mining, modern era of computers and lightning speed communication. We are currently witnessing the dawn of a new technological age where people feel lost and vulnerable if they leave their house without a mobile phone. One day, very soon, we may all be chipped and pinned. Artificial Intelligence is most definitely here to stay!

Our story is largely set during a time when women couldn't even go to a pub. They were excluded from working down the pit and there was a split between the hard physical work that was required of men and the different, often daunting domestic tasks visited upon women.

We hope this tale tells something of the seismic shifts in social history. We hope it offers you, our dear reader,

Women on the picket line during the 1984–85 Miners' Strike.

the chance to reflect on what it means to be Welsh and what it means to be a man in this ever-changing world that now openly discusses toxic masculinity and identity politics.

Times have definitely changed, old industries have completely disappeared and the future is, as always, in the hands of the young. Gone are the days when you could go out and happily leave the back door open with the money for the insurance man on the kitchen table. Gone are the days when you made an ashtray at school to take home to your mam. Gone are the days when you took a trip up the garden to use the toilet with carefully cut strips of newspaper, and gone are the days when you took turns in a tin bath.

This is a story about an ordinary miner whose mantra is still 'Once a miner always a miner', a man who calls himself part of a dying breed of men. A proud Valleys boy who says:

'Maybe I was born to help the people of the community, who knows?

'I have rescued animals.

'I have rescued people.

'I have rescued my belongings.

'I have come to realise I was put on this earth to serve the people I love.

'Or is that what being Welsh is all about?'

I will always remember the first time I met Gyp. I had recently come out of hospital and was going through a tough time. I heard about Caerau Men's Shed so I went along to Caerau Development Trust and there he was, all six-foot-four of him. 'How are you butty? Come on in.'

Now around four years later here we are, the best of butties!

Gyp has become my family. He has a heart of gold and it always amazes me to hear everyone say amazing things about him. I'm so glad that I have Gyp in my life; he has the unique ability to make you smile, even when days are tough.

I will be forever grateful that I have a friend in Chris 'Gyp' Davies.'

Owain White @Caerau Men's Shed

What's in a name?

OUR STORY IS about this man called Christopher 'Gyp' Davies. It's about the tales his life has to tell.

Like everyone else he is a flawed man with a lifetime of mistakes to look back on. His story should be told to help us all place ourselves in our history and our community. It is a time lived just after the Second World War and a time when the big industries, like mining, were brutally ended. It is a story told about one small, heavily-populated corner of south Wales. This tale should be told so we can all consider the question:

'What have I done with my life and what more could I do?'

It should be told so we can begin to discuss the meaning of the Welsh words *hiraeth* and *cynefin*.

Hiraeth = the longing for home when far away... *homesickness*.

Cynefin = a place or the time when we instinctively belong or feel most connected... *home place*.

Gyp's whole family have lived within a few streets of each other for many years, his parents grew up and spent their whole lives a stone's throw away from his current house. He is rooted; he belongs and is connected to the place. He is a Nantyffyllon boy through and through.

We will discuss this further but we had better begin by dealing with this troublesome name Gyp. It has caused some controversy. That word is definitely not a Welsh one; in fact it carries a huge weight of persecution, negativity and racism. We are treading on dangerous territory. So it is a good and necessary story to start us off. It will, and should, spark debate.

His real name is Christopher Davies but he is known by everyone as Gyp and he has a tattoo to that effect on his arm. If you visit the valley and ask to see Christopher Davies people will look at you unsure, but if you say you're looking for Gyp, almost everyone will point you in the right direction. Some would undoubtedly take issue with this nickname as being politically incorrect and an affront to gypsies and Roma Travellers. I will confess to being uncomfortable about it myself, but it is an integral part of his identity and the origins of that troublesome nickname need to be understood and, more crucially, discussed.

The reason he is called Gyp goes back to his childhood and does involve Travellers who visited and entranced a very young boy in the Llynfi Valley.

It's probably best to hear it from the man himself. Here's what he says about how he got his name:

'My name Gyp Davies came from the time when gypsies used to regularly come around the doors of Nantyffyllon, the village where I lived. This was in the 1950s and '60s.

'There was one very dark-skinned gypsy with a jet-black ponytail. He used to take our knives and sharpen them on a kerbstone for a few pennies. I befriended him as a young boy and his name was Credi.

'He told me once that if I crossed his palm with silver he would tell me my future. He told me I would need to

Gyp's primary school class… he's the tall boy in the middle of the back row.

place a silver sixpence in his right palm for him to be able to tell all.

'It was a lot of money for a small boy in the 1960s, so I did errands until I had saved up enough. I then waited and waited for Credi to visit.

'And sure enough, eventually he turned up and I placed the silver sixpence in his palm and he told me this: "You will become a great leader and be loved by many but this will weigh heavily on your heart because your heart will be so laden with love."

'In the school playground the children used to call me Gyp and say that Credi was my father. When I was in my teens I too grew a long black ponytail. I have been known all over Wales as Gyp Davies; they even used to put my name down in rugby programmes as Gyp Davies and I have agreed with my family that when I pass away my name, Gyp Davies, will be on my headstone. It is the name people have come to know and, hopefully, love.'

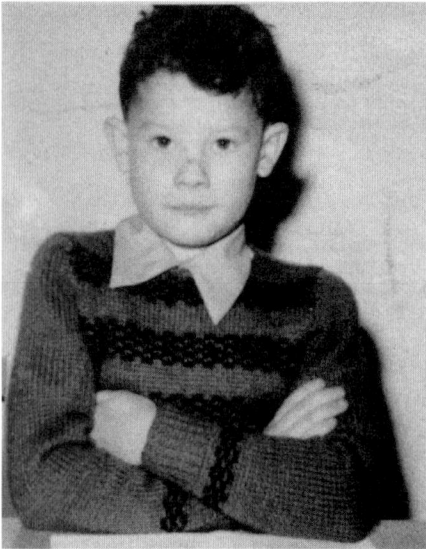

Gyp at primary school.

I'm sure this explanation won't please everyone and there are always detractors, but the story illustrates the honest and humble beginnings of the name and the man. You could argue it isn't an insult to Travellers and that it is in fact quite the opposite, it's more a mark of respect and admiration for the tinker who told him his future.

And what a leader Gyp has turned out to be, as well as a man 'so laden with love' that he has struggled with depression and is open to talking about it. The words spoken all those years ago by a Traveller have stayed with him and haunt him still.

Now cynics might suggest Credi was just making an extra sixpence from an impressionable young boy of about six or seven years old. Yet the experience left an indelible mark on Christopher Davies and christened him for a lifetime of leadership and love. Gyp believes in the telling of his fortune, and remains true to that fortune teller.

The question remains regarding the word Gyp... is it a pejorative term, should it be avoided at all costs?

The trouble is Christopher Davies has adopted it as his name out of pure respect and love for the man he looked up to as a young boy. Other children christened him with it because of his positive association with the Travellers. Christopher is definitely intending to punch up, and not down, at Roma Travellers. They have suffered enormously as an ethnic group. The Nazis killed as many as 220,000 Roma people in the Second World War. That is a story that has not been told enough.

There is a lot of talk about being woke and political correctness; language is so important and can be so loaded with prejudice to put people down. Here's what the writer Neil Gaiman said about political correctness recently:

'I was reading a book which included the phrase "in these days of political correctness..." talking about no longer making jokes that denigrated people for their culture or for the colour of their skin. And I thought – That's not actually anything to do with political correctness. That's just treating other people with respect.

'I started imagining a world in which we replaced the phrase "politically correct" wherever we could with "treating other people with respect" and it made me smile. You should try it. It's peculiarly enlightening. I know what you're thinking now. You're thinking, "Oh my god, that's treating other people with respect gone mad."'

Christopher Davies has nothing but respect and

admiration for gypsies and Roma Travellers. As noted, his adopted nickname has been used in rugby programmes and he wants it on his tombstone, but is it reinforcing that pejorative stereotype?

For the purposes of this book, we'll just stick with Gyp. It is a nigh-on-impossible task to get the people of his valley to stop using that name. It's an even greater impossible task to try and get Christopher Davies himself to stop using it; it is a crucial part of his identity. I can't use the quotes from all his friends and colleagues without including their actual words that use that nickname. I also know that anyone talking in a derogatory manner about gypsies and Roma Travellers in front of Christopher Davies will be told in no uncertain terms that it's totally unacceptable.

As he says: 'I'm proud to be called Gyp after gypsies, otherwise I would never have let that name stick. My memory of gypsies is all good. I thought they were a special kind of people. I got excited when I saw them. If I'm honest, I was in awe of them.'

Ultimately we decided to offer all the evidence we had to you, dear reader, so that you can make up your own mind about the use of the term 'Gyp'.

We will stick with 'Gyp' throughout this book because it is integral to Christopher Davies' identity and it's hard to tell his story without it!

I've known Gyp a long, long time but it's only in the last couple of years I've learnt his real name. He told me he was called Gyp because he was born under a caravan. He wasn't always meek and mild. I don't know how many red cards

Gyp in full flight playing for Nantyffyllon RFC against Aberavon in the 1980s. There was a massive brawl during this game… according to Gyp!

he had playing rugby, but if you played against him he'd definitely give you a dig.

Everybody knows him. I don't think there's a more popular man in the valley. I persuaded him to stand as a county councillor because he has such a following. And anyone refereeing a game with Gyp in would certainly have a red stain on their fingers.

I remember a Cup game against Glyncorrwg and a fight started and it was the fifteen men from each side brawling. I was standing next to their coach who said, 'I thought we were playing rugby,' and I had to turn away as I knew it was Gyp who'd started it.

Tom Beedle @Caerau Men's Shed

Roots

IT'S IRONIC THAT some people get so passionate and raise the clarion call of 'As long as we beat the English!'

But, of course, the reality is a little more blurred for every one of us. We're all travellers and migrants and there are no 'pedigree' Welsh people as far as I know. How would we all view the world if there was an acceptance, proven by history, in which we're all travellers and migrants? I saw the BBC broadcaster Roy Noble recently, who went so far as to say that anyone in south Wales who claims to be pure thoroughbred Welsh is a liar!

Roy has very kindly written the foreword for this book and believes Gyp's story is wrapped up in bigger tales of migration and belonging.

There are some people living in parts of the world that will become uninhabitable in the next fifty years because of global warming. They will migrate out of desperation and necessity, but some commentators suggest we should begin planning for that mass migration now, building new cities to house sixty million from desert wastelands and other sinking lands. Can you imagine any politician trying to stand on a platform of accommodating people into new urban conurbations?

In terms of identity, is Hanan Issa, appointed as the National Poet of Wales, a proud Welsh-Iraqi woman? Of course she is, and long may she remain so!

That's not saying that people shouldn't understand the colonial rule imposed in all corners of the United Kingdom, and elsewhere in the world, by an English ruling class.

As Gyp says: 'It never seems to be ordinary working people who ruthlessly exploit each other for monetary gain. Throughout history working people have, more often than not, stuck together to fight for their lives and livelihoods.'

Gyp's roots come from far and wide and bring a thousand stories to the table. He is passionately and fiercely Welsh but he'd never claim to be thoroughbred Welsh. His family might be rooted in Nantyffyllon now but, delve back into anyone's past, it won't be long before you'll find migrants and movers.

His greater family are all travellers of one sort or another. They herald from Bath and Brecknockshire and his family have some impressive claims to fame. Gyp knows Wales has always been an ethnically diverse nation and he believes we should always celebrate that fact.

Cedric Bassett Popkin is often credited with having shot down the famous Red Baron fighter pilot during the First World War. Cedric's family were originally from

Cedric Bassett Popkin, a member of Gyp's family who allegedly shot down the Red Baron fighter pilot.

37

Maesteg, belonging to Gyp's great-grandmother, Annie Alice Popkin. That side of the family emigrated to Australia and became yet another family of migrants and travellers too.

Digging deeper again, we know that it was one shot from the ground that was fatal for Baron von Richthofen and that historical research gives us three possible shooters that day. We're going to use poetic licence for Gyp and claim Popkin got him! The trajectory of the bullet, according to scientists, favours the Popkin theory.

On another side of his family, his great-grandfather was a sea captain who won a silver medal for bravery.

Here's what Gyp says about it: 'On 7th January 1839 a ship bound from Swansea to Dublin with coal got stranded in the shallows near Port Talbot. One of the crew was an excellent swimmer and reached the shore and reported that the ship was breaking up. Captain Charles Sutton, along with others, rowed out through heavy seas to the wreck. Onlookers on the beach thought the little boat had herself been lost and, just when she did reach the wreck, a sudden wave washed all four men temporarily overboard and smashed most of the oars. The little boat was then washed up on the beach.

'After a change of clothing and a short rest they rowed out again. For the second time they were washed overboard and, clinging to the boat and the oars, they were washed back to the beach again, badly bruised.

'A third rescue attempt was then made and this time they were successful in rescuing the master of the sinking ship and four crew members. Unfortunately, three crew members had already been lost at sea.

'The silver medal was awarded to Captains Jones, Howell, Sutton and Foley and to the pilots Lewis Jenkins and Arthur Rees. Other rescuers received awards of cash.'

So there you have it, Gyp is from brave and heroic stock, including the very unique man that was his father. He plays a very significant role in this story alongside his wife, Gyp's mam.

Gyp's father, Daniel Davies, was at Dunkirk during the Second World War. He was only a young man then of about twenty years old. The whole British Expeditionary Force had been pushed to the shores of France and the Germans were bombing the boats as they arrived to rescue people. It wasn't just soldiers either; the townspeople too were trying to escape.

Danny (Gyp's father) was with other soldiers in a lorry but, as they approached the beach, they all had to jump out as they were being shot at by a Messerschmitt fighter plane. Danny ran down the street and dived into a wine cellar to save himself but, unfortunately, he didn't anticipate the twenty-foot drop into the cellar and he broke his leg. He would later tell his son Gyp that it was that wine cellar that saved his life because breaking his leg made him an injured casualty and it guaranteed him a place on the boat home.

He still had to make his way back to the beach, avoiding more gunfire, and then he had to climb the netting up the side of a big ship with all the pain of his broken leg.

When Danny returned home it was all too much for

him and he had what Gyp describes as an emotional breakdown and was admitted to hospital. Nowadays we would call it Post-Traumatic Stress Disorder. Everything that he had seen played on his mind and he couldn't shake it off for the rest of his days. He had witnessed good friends shot down next to him and other terrible atrocities that he never wanted to share.

Gyp asked his sister to explain it further and this is what he told me: 'My sister said the reason my father was in a mental hospital after Dunkirk is because his friend was standing next to him on that rescue ship and had his head blown off by a lump of flying shrapnel while they were being attacked. It could so easily have been my father, they were standing so close together. He had the trauma and the guilt of it being his friend and not him all his life. How do you get over that?'

His war was over and eventually he went back to work in the pit and stayed there for another thirty-plus years.

Danny Davies took to the drink and there were times in Gyp's childhood when things were not easy. He has an enduring respect for his sister, June, who is twelve years older than him. She protected him and shielded him from his father's worst excesses.

Earlier in his life his sister also stood in for Gyp's mother when she experienced post-natal depression and struggled to bond with her son. His sister would come home from school at lunchtimes to bathe him and dress him. She stepped in to help her mother to look after her little brother.

Gyp now acknowledges that his mother suffered with

Gyp's parents during the war years.

depression, but life was so hard and all women had to hold everything together. It is a painful experience for Gyp to recall those childhood memories.

There was not the understanding or the help around for people back in those days... life could be very tough. Mental health and well-being were not terms that were readily bandied around like they are now, there was a stigma and there was a sense of guilt and shame. Anyone who couldn't cope was seen to be exhibiting weakness.

He's a fucking nutcase! I've known him for fifty years and worked at the paper mill with him. He fought for everyone. He literally helped everybody. The bloke is a legend. One of the nicest blokes I've ever met.

I was a first-aider in the mill and one day he asked me to look at his arm. He said he'd been at the rugby club at

41

the weekend and had a skinful, then went home and fell asleep on the radiator. He said he woke up thinking he could smell beef burgers, but it was his flesh burning. He lifted his arm off and left half his skin behind, but he was so tough he didn't feel it.

Dai Womble @Caerau Men's Shed

A union man

WE LIVE IN an ever-changing world.

Gyp grew into his working life with a deep understanding of the importance of trade unions. His father was a union man and people came to the house for his advice and support. His father told him that with his first pay packet the most important thing he could do was join the union.

Gyp's father was the vice chair of the National Union of Mineworkers (NUM). On a Sunday he remembers his father would spend the afternoon helping miners fill in compensation forms. Gyp marvelled at the respect people had for his father and how appreciative they were of what he did for them, even though Gyp never really understood at that stage exactly what was going on.

As Gyp says, being a miner and a union man is 'in my blood'. It has shaped his whole life and their issues affect the whole family, the whole community. His father, his grandfather and his uncles were all miners. For Gyp it's a part of what being Welsh should be as we are all a product of that history and that struggle for working people's rights. Gyp remains passionate to this day about the coal mining industry and its heritage and what it means to Wales.

We are now living in an age when Labour Party politicians are disciplined for standing on a picket line...

The 1984–85 strike… off to picket.

this is the very same Labour Party that was formed by and for working-class people to ensure they had a vote and a voice in the corridors of power!

Gyp himself became head of a union after he left the mines and began work at the Maesteg Paper Mill. He was awarded a silver medal of merit for being the union rep for thirty years, in what is now known as the Unite union. He was also awarded the President's Safety Award for the most hours without an accident in the mill (250,000 work hours, accident-free).

Gyp readily admits he was a thorn in the management's side for all those years. He jokingly said that, when he left, the managers probably threw a party. He was also a hard worker and a grafter. He had, most crucially, the backing of all the men. If he said to shut down the machines, then the machines would shut down without question.

Marching for their livelihoods.

Sometimes it was because of wages and sometimes it was because of safety reasons. He made sure that workers were entitled to sick pay for up to three months and then he got that extended to a year.

He had no agenda and no ego. Gyp was genuinely all about fighting for the rights of his fellow workers. He knew there were many in the mill who couldn't read or write, so Gyp became the learning rep and he made sure those who needed help could get it and move themselves forward, and all in the strictest confidence.

If workers had accidents at work, then Gyp would visit them and hear their needs and concerns.

He visited one man in hospital in Swansea after he'd had a nasty accident, injuring his legs. The man told Gyp they wouldn't let him home from the hospital until his house had handrails leading up to it and inside.

45

Gyp confronted a manager about this and the manager replied, 'Well what do you want me to do about it?'

Gyp brought his huge bear-like hands thumping down on the table in reply and boomed, 'I WANT YOU TO SHOW SOME FUCKING COMPASSION!'

The manager flinched and pens went flying through the air and Gyp broke his little finger in the process.

Needless to say, the fitters and woodworkers in the plant made the rails and fitted them the next day. The handrails are still outside that house to this day.

The management marvelled at how popular Gyp was with the workers. They even asked him why the men trusted him so much more than management.

Gyp replied in true fashion: 'I know what each and every one of them has in their sandwiches each day.'

He then pointed at a worker as he walked by: 'See him. That's Brian and he'll have cheese and onion.'

The management bought into the myth of the man, although Gyp tells me now he didn't have a clue what Brian had in his sandwiches. The point was that Gyp really did know the men and stood by them at all times and stood up to management on their behalf… and every one of them knew that.

To this day Gyp cannot understand workers not gathering together, bargaining collectively and belonging to a trade union.

He was a good rugby player. He played for Maesteg. In his first game he was on for three minutes before he got sent off! His motto was 'Don't worry about the ball, play the game.'

Gyp himself is a rare breed. He has been very down and he's been really depressed. He really piled on the weight at one time but then fought back and got himself back fit and strong. He is a fighter. He's like the Pied Piper in some ways because lots of men have followed him down to Billy's Gym and we all work out now when we can.

Councillor Gwyn Williams @Caerau Men's Shed

Mining

GYP GREW UP with mining.

Even as a young boy he remembers he would go with his mates and knock on the door of the man in his street that bred canaries for the pits in the valley. The chance to see exotic birds was irresistible for a group of young children, despite their reluctance to engage with a gruff old man in their neighbourhood!

Gyp tells the story: 'His name was Griff Petty and he was a rough customer. He was a big bloke with a big beard and a waistcoat. He looked intimidating. We were frightened of him really but we knocked the door and he let us in and we'd go out the back garden where he had all the canaries.

'I think he liked our company and was a bit lonely as he lived on his own and he didn't have much. He had been married. He didn't want us to go. He'd make us sandwiches with vinegar in. We all looked at each other with faces of disgust but none of us would say anything 'cos we was fucking frightened of him. Now you'd think we'd have said, "Well we won't go back there with his vinegar sandwiches and him so scary an' all." But we went back for more and knocked his door again and again.'

When Gyp left school at the age of fifteen he headed straight for the pit. The year was 1970 and these were the days of Woolworths, Brut aftershave; Black Sabbath, Angel Delight, T. Rex, Hai Karate and 'The Ballroom Blitz'.

As Gyp remembers: 'I remember picking my first pay packet up – you had to queue in a long line and the clerk would pass your pay packet through the window: "Davies CL," he said, "It's £7.50!"'

'Well I can't tell you how it felt to be earning a weekly wage. There was a pub just through the tunnel from the

Miners caring for the pit horses.

The appalling working conditions underground.

pit called The Dyffryn, so I was straight in there with my butties after we had showered. We had a pint, all under age mind, and we were discussing what we were going to spend our pay on.

'Anyway in those first few weeks I decided to give my

mam £5 towards the bills and keep £2.50 for myself. After a few pints we always jumped on the bus to town [Maesteg]. Every Friday, town was packed in the 1970s; there were plenty of wages to be spent back in those days.

'One of my very first pounds was put down as a deposit for a Levi jacket in Gwynne's clothes shop. I was to pay every week for it; I think it cost £5 in total, that left me £1.50 for the rest of the week. In those days a pint was about 11p. There were discos in the town hall at the weekend. There were flagons to be drunk in the old garage on the school hill. We wore platform shoes, Paisley shirts, flared jeans or herringbone trousers. We had longer hair back then and I had a moustache!

'And we'd try and do a bit of courting (polite version) in between the fighting, LOL. The 1970s were magic if you were a sixteen or seventeen year old.'

He didn't go straight down the pit though, that wasn't the way. Young lads started at the top of the pit, working on the timber or working in the stables.

Gyp remembers trying to put a collar on a horse; he thought you had to get the horse to step into it. After struggling with a very reluctant animal for half an hour, he learnt to his cost from an experienced collier that he had it upside down and you fitted the collar over the head of the horse. It gave all the boys watching a really good laugh and Gyp took stick for that for a while afterwards.

He also remembers the rats in the stables. He would catch them alive and sell them to the old colliers who had Jack Russell dogs. They used to throw six rats in the back of an empty coal lorry and then put their dog in there to sort them out. Gyp would be paid 50p for three live rats.

I couldn't resist asking him how he caught them and his answer was: 'A Mars bar and a bucket! I'd turn the bucket upside down and prop it up with a stick on a string. They loved the Mars bar but sometimes I had to wait ages for them. I upgraded to KiteKat afterwards. I knew the fat cat at the pit wouldn't move to eat it.'

Gyp also had the job of taking the horses to the field when the pit was closed for miners' fortnight. He says: 'It was great to see them galloping about and rolling on the floor, kicking their back legs high in the air. They were free for a short while.'

At the end of that fortnight though, he admits it was really hard work to get them back in the stables. It was another old collier who showed him the trick of how to do it... with a bag of sherbet lemons!

The horses had very tough lives, being underground for so long and hardly experiencing daylight, but the colliers looked after them with as much care and compassion as they could and the bond between them was strong. The same could not be said for the rats in the stables.

At sixteen Gyp went down the pit and was paired with an experienced collier called Robert Thomas, who was really good to Gyp and taught him so much. Gyp is a hefty man but he described Robert as 'a big ginger collier with muscles in his ears'. He watched him in awe. The two of them still meet up to this day.

It was from watching Robert that Gyp got to

understand his father's blue scars. Many miners have blue scars where they worked with their shirts off and coal dust became ingrained under their skin, particularly if they had an open cut or scratch. Gyp's father had them on his arms, his face and his back. The miners often had their shirts off because then they could feel the dust fall on them and this might save their lives if the roof was about to come down.

Gyp can recall the first time he really noticed his father's blue scars. He says: 'My father used to have a shave out the back. It wasn't a proper bathroom back then; it was a single breeze block room with asbestos sheets. It was fucking freezing in there. It was the same bath out there that we bathed in and where my father also killed the chickens.

'I remember when I was about ten or eleven years old and he was stripped to the waist shaving. His back was very muscular but he had these blue marks all over his back and on his shoulders too.

'I asked him: "Dad what's those blue marks on your back?" And he said: "Aw, that's from when I fought a tiger, son."

'"Did you win Dad?" I asked him.

'"Aye son, I did, and I've still got the teeth to prove it.'

'At that age I was so excited by what he'd told me that I couldn't wait to go out and tell my butties. I gathered them all around and told them my father had fought a tiger and beat it. They all believed it too and we all retold the story everywhere.

'It was only years later that I realised you'd never find a tiger in Nanty. It was then I realised what they really were and why my father had the scars on his face and on his eyes… poor bugger.'

On his first day at the face, Gyp had to crawl and push his way through a very narrow, tight, water-filled gap on his hands and knees with the coal dust so thick you couldn't see your hand in front of you. It was too much for another new starter; he was too afraid and so was taken back up and left the pit. Gyp also felt an urge to turn and go too, but his dad was his hero and, as a matter of pride, he knew he couldn't run away. He was aware, as all miners were, that the whole of Glamorgan was pressing down upon them as they worked.

Even the initiation ceremonies were tough. Gyp remembers being a bit of a cocky youngster, leaving school and thinking he was a cool cookie going down the mine. But as he often says, the tough old colliers would take you down a peg or two if needed, as lives depended on everyone pulling together.

Gyp's initiation is one he hasn't forgotten and certainly brought him down to earth (eventually!). One break-time in a small cavern, they hooked him up to the rigging by his belt and hoisted him up about twenty feet in the air to the roof arches and then they just left him hanging there for hours. He couldn't even pee and he had to urinate in his trousers up in the air. He wasn't quite such a Jack the Lad after that and learnt his place in the pecking order.

Mining was a hard job and men didn't a need gym membership back in those days, the work toned them and made them physically very strong and tough.

As Gyp comments: 'There was a time that working on the coal face made me so strong that my party trick was to bend six-inch nails with my bare hands. Many boys left the pit too because it was such hard physical work.'

But those who remained were bonded together by the work, as Gyp says: 'Men stuck together in adverse times, strikes come to mind as a perfect example. We played sport together, we socialised together, we sang together and we holidayed together. It was all about togetherness. It was all about comradeship. When things were tough we all had each other's backs. It might sound corny but we were a very real band of brothers.

'Would you carry your butty who was injured in a fall two miles underground to safety? If you were a miner the answer is always YES!'

When he was a young sixteen-year-old miner on his first day at the seam, Gyp saw an older man working next to him crushed by a slab that fell on top of him from above. He survived but both his lungs were punctured.

People lost limbs and people died and you always had to fight for any compensation. The managers would always make out the accident was your own fault.

There was another occasion when a miner working alongside Gyp prodded him and said, 'Go and wake up Dai. I think he's fallen asleep.' Gyp dutifully crawled over to the next bay and Dai was on his knees slumped forward with his shovel in his hand. Gyp shook him but he didn't wake up... he was dead. Gyp then helped to carry him on a stretcher about a mile-and-a-half to get him out of the pit.

Gyp's father had an accident when he was notching timber and cut right through his boot and sliced his big toe almost right off. The men carried him out and he was stitched up. He was taken home on a horse because of bad snow, but in those days no work meant no money. Often men would go back to work when they weren't right.

Gyp tells the story of a miner who struggled to make ends meet: 'I had a butty in the pit and he came from a poor family, his mam had loads of kids, so every penny was important to him. I used to give him my old clothes that were two sizes too big for him but he wore them anyway. He always had immaculate black boots; he'd spend hours polishing them. The rest of him was a bag of shite but his boots – well you could see your face in them.

"'Look at my boots Gyp," he'd say and I'd say, "Aye, I know butty." He was so proud of them boots. Anyway, one day he says to me: "I have to dump my boots, Gyp."

"'Why?" I asked.

"'There's a big hole in them, in the top by my big toe. Can you lend me 50p to get a new pair?"

"'You won't get a new pair for 50p, butty," I told him.

"'I will mun," he said. "You watch and see now Gyp."

'The next shift he comes over and says, "Hey look at my boots Gyp, they're like new."

"'Did you manage to get a pair for 50p then?" I asked him.

"'No mun, look closer," he says.

"I looked down and I could see his big toe with no sock on it. He'd sprayed his toe black so it blended in with his boot.

"'It's valley magic Gyp," he said.'

Every time I talk to Gyp another story eases from him

and I'm sure if I spent another ten years compiling this book I still wouldn't exhaust his entire repertoire. Any topic brings another round of recollections.

Gyp also tells of the times when you worked in different districts and you might have to walk a mile underground before you reached the coal. It was possible to walk from Aberbargoed to Crumlin underground. If it was an old coal face you might have to walk bent over the whole way because the roof was so low.

He talks of how his father died eventually from dust on the lungs. He says: 'Pneumoconiosis is one of a group of lung diseases caused by breathing in certain kinds of dust particles that can damage your lungs. It takes years to develop.

'My dad's lungs were fucked. He used to cough up black and blood stuff into a vessel and say, "Look that's what being a collier does to you, boy!"'

Gyp says his father was determined not to die until he had his 'dust money' from the government. His father often said to him, 'They're waiting for us all to die off so they don't have to pay up, but I'm not going till I get mine.'

He did get the money, then died from the pneumoconiosis.

It was a hard man's world.

The well-known strikes of 1972, 1974 and 1984 were huge moments in British history and signalled the eventual end of the coal mining industry in Britain.

It wasn't for any environmental reasons; it was a political attack by the government to end any power the trade union movement had. Coal was king, so the

Solidarity is a weapon

'Solidarity is a weapon' is self-explanatory – an apt phrase but a far cry from today's zero hours contracts and the minimum wage culture of the 'gig economy'.

NUM was the union the government wanted to defeat so workers would be weakened and, once again, at the mercy of unscrupulous bosses.

It is the world we now live in where so many workers are on minimum wage and zero hours contracts. Many workers now are not in trade unions and those that are face severe restrictions on wielding any real power for their members.

Gyp had left the mines before the 1984 strike and followed his father by going to work at the Maesteg paper mill. The money was better and the work was a lot easier.

During the 1984 strike Gyp continued to do all he could for the striking miners. He took people out and looked after them. He knew his friends at the pit were friends for life. He stood with them on the picket line whenever he could.

He saw someone recently who reminded Gyp of the time he had bought him his first pair of Adidas trainers. It was during the 1984 miners' strike when he was a young boy and his striking family had no money. The man, much older now, has never forgotten Gyp for that.

Gyp took many in and fed them during that time but he sees that as everything good that a community does... more than that, it's what community is!

He knew some of those miners were drunks and wife-beaters but they all had children and those children couldn't be held responsible and had to be helped.

The 1984 strike was a crucial life-and-death issue, both for communities and for some miners.

Alan Williams, who is part of the Llynfi Valley Ex-Miners' Group where Gyp is the chair, told me a story from the 1984 strike that is not widely known: 'During the 1984 strike the unloading cranes at Port Talbot steelworks were used to unload all the imported coal and stockpile it at the steelworks. It was all about undermining the strike.

'So we, illegally, took over the cranes for a weekend. We wanted to show everybody how much imported coal was coming in. So 108 of us went down to the steelworks and took over the cranes. We climbed up and were 208 feet up. We took up five rolls of barbed wire, thirty-eight gallons of water and 500 tins of food. But we only had eight mugs between us all so we ended up drinking tea out of empty bean tins!

Miner arrested during the 1984 strike.

'The *Argos* ship was doing its maiden voyage from Spain with 98,000 tons of coal on that one ship. That vessel stayed beneath us for the weekend and could not unload. By the time we all came down there were eleven ships queuing up in the sea, so you can imagine the amount of coal coming in, and we made an impact and made a point that weekend.

'But the story had a tragic side too. When we came down there were 108 police officers waiting for us, one for every miner. They arrested us all and we were charged with unlawful assembly and criminal damage. The unlawful assembly charge carried a prison term. It was subsequently agreed that if we pleaded guilty to criminal damage they would drop the unlawful assembly charge. But before that deal was made there was one young miner who couldn't bear the thought of going to prison and he committed suicide.

'So 108 of us turned up for the first court case but only 107 of us actually got sentenced. We were given a two-year suspended sentence and it was all for trying to save our jobs really.'

There was enormous pain in all the south Wales communities during that year of 1984–85. The government used all its power to win the strike and defeat the miners. The battle at Orgreave in Yorkshire has been well documented, with evidence to support the notion that the police were used as a weapon of the state against their own people, actively working to systematically undermine and destroy the spirit and resolve of the miners, using tactics that were, at times, highly dubious. Gyp is convinced that in south Wales too there were people in police uniform on the picket line who weren't actually policemen.

Leighton Thomas, a retired miner from Nantymoel and a naturally shy man, gave me an account of what happened to him that supports Gyp's notion of bogus officers. This is what Leighton told me:

'I was on the picket line during the strike and there were soldiers there wearing unmarked police uniforms. One particular "soldier/policeman" kicked the shins of miners with his boots, trying to provoke them. A miner I knew took exception to that and said, "If he's back here again tomorrow I'm going to have him."

'He was back the next day and the miner reached over

the top of me and punched him. I was then pulled from the line and arrested for assaulting the officer. I had never broken the law in my life. In the police station I was scared and was made to wait for hours. Eventually an NUM union official came and got me bail.

'I subsequently went to court and was fined £50 and bound over. I now have a criminal record. I stood up in court and said, "That officer giving evidence about me for supposedly assaulting him is definitely not the same officer who was actually assaulted on the day in question." They took no notice.

'It was obvious to me that the aggressive officer who was punched was not a policeman at all and had been drafted in like so many others to do a job on the miners. A regular policeman then had to lie on oath and pretend he was the policeman assaulted that day.'

The 1984 strike was well supported in Wales and Gyp remembers some miners who were too proud to take hand-outs, but then people took it round when they weren't in and left it on the doorstep. They were tough times of real hardship when people fought for their livelihoods and their communities.

Where are all those miners now with the pits all gone? What became of all those wasted lives?

There is limited research into what became of all those miners. What research is available highlights the lack of planning for the pit closures, in part because the battle to defeat the unions was, first and foremost, the principal objective of the government. Those politicians and officials had absolutely no regard for the complete and wilful destruction of whole communities.

A report by the Global Subsidies Initiative found that there were key lessons to learn from what happened in south Wales. Those lessons, the report says, would be vital elsewhere in the world if another area was in danger of losing its core industry. It would require a 'comprehensive response'. Such a response didn't happen in south Wales and so nothing was in place to alleviate the pain experienced by those communities:

'Despite the inability of policy to offset the social impacts of industrial decline in south Wales... A key finding is the need to develop a comprehensive response that includes measures that generate economic activity, improve infrastructure, maintain social cohesion and establish effective institutions to implement the response.'
(*The End of Coal Mining in South Wales: Lessons learned from industrial transformation* (2017), Global Subsidies Initiative)

There was no planning and there were no 'comprehensive' measures in south Wales and the whole area was left to flounder and decay.

There is evidence that, following pit closures, people relied on social welfare payments and were still relying on those payments two decades on, which points to the conclusion by the Global Subsidies Initiative report that:
'... in the case of south Wales this support [government support] has not proved sufficient to create a resilient and diverse economy in the longer term.'

The evidence is there that despite the best efforts of bodies like the WDA (Welsh Development Agency), the valleys of south Wales were left battered and broken by the closure of the industry that was their lifeblood. The

63

after-effects and the ripples of that are still being felt to this day.

What remains are the stories of men like Gyp. We may not know what became of all those miners but he holds on to the memories of some of them and the memories of all that banter and camaraderie. He still believes in that very real sense of belonging and community.

He has hope.

He still recalls many of the nicknames the miners gave each other. It was an integral part of the ritual of going underground together and maintaining that togetherness. He gave me this list of names he could remember, and these were the name-tags of real men who worked in the Llynfi Valley pits:

Will Silent; Will Be Tidy; Roy Watch & Chain; Cyril Jumping Chalk; Dai Bible; Dai Rubs; Dai Stick a Fork; Dai Slam and Bang; Ifor Slack Rope; Up and Down; Cap and Gown; Alf Shamfer; Billy Fall Down; Ronny Suck and Blow; Jimmy Snobs; Jimmy Black Shed; Eggs on Legs; Bulb Eyes; Billy Go Deeper; Edwin Large Fag; Dick Cawl; Dancing Taff; Des Small Bit; Mervyn Tuppence Off; Mini Miner; Terry Tide Mark; Sel Still Hanging; Derrick Dampers.

These are just the ones he took time to recall... there were many others, including of course... Gyp Davies!

There was a point when Gyp and his mate 'Trouty' wanted to insert a whole chapter entitled 'Fifty Shades of Dai'.

They reckoned they knew fifty different Dai nicknames that they'd worked with over the years. But I had to draw the line somewhere and said we couldn't do it.

'But Churchy,' said Gyp, 'What about Dai Twice?'

I said, 'Why was he called Dai Twice?'

'Because his real name was David David... and then there was Dai Small Spuds because he always complained the potatoes were too small in the canteen. There was Dai Bungalow 'cos there was nothing much upstairs, and Dai Up and Down because he had one leg shorter than the other.

'We're not doing it, Gyp!'

'But what about Dai Tombstone who used to inscribe the memorials at Maesteg Cemetery or Dai Bambi who was always falling over, and then there was Dai Dirty Curtains who was called that because he was always complaining that other people in the street never washed their curtains... and Dai Cardboard Back because he always complained his back was bad to get out of lifting jobs but we all saw him lifting heavy logs in his back garden.'

'I'm still not convinced,' I say.

Thankfully I steer the conversation away from fifty shades and back to the mines. It's when we really talk about the pits and their communities that Gyp really gets going and talks to me with a passion about the past and the future.

As he says: 'We should never forget how the Valleys were forged and made from coal and iron. We should remember the men who toiled with their blood, sweat and tears to put food and a roof over the heads of their families. They fought to survive. Now they are a dying breed of superhuman beings, beasts who crawled below ground to earn a living.

'They are LEGENDS and they must never be forgotten.

'Look up to the mountains and see the scars of a bygone age when coal was king. I was one of many and when we miners pass each other in the streets today we remember that time and just a simple nod between us will be enough.

'Now I see a lost generation wandering on a path to nowhere. I see some youngsters with no sense of community or belonging. But there is light at the end of the tunnel, you just have to walk towards it.

'Youngsters need employment, hope, and motivation. They need that regeneration plan that we never had when the pits closed. What motivated me was that sense of belonging I always had, those growing feelings of self-worth and the need to be loved.

'It's not going to be easy but who said it would be?'

He also wrote this and emailed it to me with a picture of the empty pit baths after we'd visited the Big Pit together. There is never any doubt that he wants to remember those mining days. His thoughts capture the times in those showers that are now no more:

There was a time

The showers are empty now
No more jokes and no more banter
No more blackened bodies wandering naked
With sponge and soap in hand
Heading for the showers
That never worked properly

Scalding your back
As you sang at the top of your voice
Songs from the Seventies
Out of tune but who cares?
No more 'Wash my back please butty
And I'll wash yours'
No more washing the coal dust from your eyes
Washing so hard it stung
No more rushing as fast as you can
Desperate not to lose drinking time in the pub
With the coal dust still clinging to you
No more 'See you at the pit bottom in the morning butty.'

It's all just memories now of days gone by
But stop a while to recall
You'll faintly hear the wheels winding again
And taste that dusty, stale air
Stop a while
You are a dying breed
Fill yourself with pride
In the legends of time
Back in the days when coal was king.

He's a gentle giant. He can be obstinate if he wants to be.
He can be confrontational but he never likes the aggro that
goes with it. Emotionally he's very sensitive. He'll come
to the house to talk things through if he's worried about
something.

He's ideal to run the Shed because he leads by example.
Nobody else could have dealt with the things he's had to
deal with. He's a social animal who needs people around

him. The pandemic was a nightmare for him because he craves the company of people to bounce off.

He's a really great bloke.

Phil 'the Flash' Davies @Caerau Men's Shed

Women

IT WOULD BE remiss of this personal history if we didn't acknowledge the role of women in mining life. Gyp was in awe of his father as a working miner but he also says: 'My father was tough but I think my mum was tougher!'

His mother came from a family of thirteen, whereas his father was an only child. They lived across the street from each other and that is how they met; they were both from deep-rooted mining families. That, in some ways, is why Gyp has been a miner his whole life and remains one to this day… it is in his blood.

His mother had a much tougher childhood than his father and Gyp recalls moments when his mother would put her husband in his place when he was moaning about his lot. She would remind him in no uncertain terms of the much tougher childhood she had endured. Her family had relied on buying cold leftover chips cheap from the chip shop, they had struggled all through her childhood and Gyp's father knew it, which is why she had the ability to silence him at times.

Gyp's admiration for his mother is very clear and he calls her his best friend. He appreciates how much she gave to hold the family together in tough times. She would often go without food to make sure everyone else could eat. The husband was the breadwinner but there was enormous pressure on a wife to run the house. Many

Gyp's mother.

miners gave their pay to their wives and it was the mothers who made things work out.

Gyp's mam was Doris Sutton who then became Doris Davies, and she was a force of nature.

She was a hugely dependable woman in the street. People came to her when they needed their dead family members laid out. A board would be laid out on the bath in Gyp's house and the body would be put there and cleaned. People also came to her when a child was stillborn. Doris just always knew what to do and was so well respected by all.

And when Gyp had begun working in the mines as a young lad, he was offered overtime one day and took it and worked on late. His mother had put out his tea on the table and young Gyp didn't appear. He hadn't let her know he was working late. There were no mobile phones back then.

So when he finished his shift and came up the shaft all the boys were looking at him and he didn't know why. Then, through a crowd of very respectful miners the little figure of his mother appeared and gave him an absolute rollicking for not turning up for his dinner. And he had to stand and take it; such was his enormous respect for his mam. Not one miner said a word either as she unleashed her powerful reproach to her son.

Of course he also took a lot of stick for it later and was often referred to as a 'mammy's boy' in the weeks that followed, such is the banter of the pits.

His mother also taught her boy never to complain about his sandwiches.

He says: 'Every grub time, when we went to have our food sitting on the floor in the pit, we'd all ask each other, "What have you got in your sandwiches today?" I always used to have ham, lettuce and tomato all the time and the others made fun of that.

'So I went home one day and said to my mam, "Mam, I'm fed up of ham, lettuce and tomato. I have them every single day."

'My mam said, "OK boy."

'The following shift it was grub time again and all the boys opened their boxes and were saying what they'd got, whether it was cheese and onion or jam or whatever.

'"What have you got Gyp?" they asked.

'"I don't know," I said.

'"Well is it ham, tomato and lettuce?"

'"No," I said, "It's something different this time."

'"Tell us then, what is it?" they demanded.

'So I bit into it and they all looked at me.

'"What's the matter Gyp?" they wanted to know.

'"It's fucking toothpaste," I said.

'So I gave the sandwiches to the horse. I went home and said, "Mam what did you put in my sandwiches?"

'"Toothpaste," she said.

'"Why did you do that?"

'"Well you won't complain about ham, lettuce and tomato again, will you!"

'She was only little, but my mam packed one hell of a punch.'

Gyp says of the women of the area: 'The women of the valley are among the strongest and most compassionate I have ever witnessed. They were the glue that held families together, especially during the miners' strikes. During the strikes they ran soup kitchens, they organised, they cooked, they managed, they consoled and they stood on the picket lines with their men. The longer the strike went on, the more the women played their part and saw it as their struggle as much as the men's.

'They were brave and beautiful, they were deadly and dutiful. When called upon, they would stand up and be counted.'

It was a tight-knit community. Everybody helped each other. You could go next door even if no one was in, and you could take bread, butter and sugar, then leave a note telling them what you'd borrowed. Everyone had virtually nothing, but they all had virtually nothing together.

When Gyp's father was coughing really badly one day, he was sent next door to get a 'fingerful of Vick'. The neighbour duly held open the jar and Gyp ran back with the Vick clinging to his finger and then rubbed it on his dad's chest.

Gyp had great respect and admiration for one memorable woman called Violet John. She was a relentless campaigner for miners during the strike in 1984.

Gyp says: 'I recently met Violet at the fifty-year anniversary of the mining museum in October 2022. I was aware of her in the 1984 strike when she and many other women were instrumental in setting up the Food for Miners programme at the Nantyffyllon Miners' Institute. She, along with other women, distributed food parcels too.

'It goes to show how strong-minded the wives, mothers and sisters of the miners were and she raised funds and awareness on their behalf. She was a determined woman who never gave up. She was the same as me in that she saw the suffering of the children during that very tough year. You couldn't help everybody but we all did the best we could to help people. So many people were really close to the breadline and some were being chucked out of their homes. They'd already sold their car and every other item they had to make ends meet and some people had nothing left.

'You have to remember miners had a fair wage coming in and when they didn't have that coming in any more they started to lose everything. The strike left a deep scar in the community and, for some, that still hasn't healed even today. For me, I believe in forgiveness but it's not easy, you have to understand the real pressures people were under back then. It affected everyone in different ways.'

The impact of the 1984 strike cannot be overstated in its effect on the south Wales Valleys and in the way it changed British trade unionism. At the time of writing this book there are numerous workers, in a wide range of occupations, going out on strike. People believe the gap between the 'haves' and the 'have nots' is now greater than it has ever been. Tax evasion and offshore banking is wholly acceptable but being in a trade union appears not to be. It is getting harder and harder as more and more obstacles are created to stop workers ever having the right to strike at all. It is not an easy time to be fighting injustice in the workplace and beyond.

A *Western Mail* newspaper journalist, recalling the 1984 strike, wrote this piece about the political awakening of those women who fought to defend the miners and about Violet John in particular: 'One of the most significant things about the strike was the way that women in the mining areas became politically active. No longer content to let the men do the fighting, the wives of miners, supported by other women, formed themselves into miners' support groups throughout south Wales. And one of the most active was in Maesteg which covered the Llynfi and Afan valleys and which supported 1,000 striking miners and their families.

'One woman who became a leading activist, not only in Maesteg but further afield, was Vi John of Garth.

'"I moved here when I married my husband Adrian who was not a miner," she said. "I'm from Northern Ireland and I was concerned about the way people were being treated by the police – it reminded me of what I saw in Ulster."

'Mrs John was present at the inaugural meeting of the support group.

'"I went along to Nantyffyllon Library where the NUM was based and offered to help," she said. "Every week the wives gathered together food donated by valley

Mining families scavenging for coal during the winter of the 1984–85 strike.

residents and others – and also purchased items with money donated to ensure that people didn't go hungry.

'"We had 100 per cent support from people in Maesteg," she recalled. "The whole valley was in the fight. I used to go out collecting around the factories and streets and everyone gave... People had nothing."

'Mrs John devoted her whole energy to the strike for that year, and from the November ran a soup kitchen in Garth. "By then the men had been out for six months," she said. "The weather was getting cold and people had used up their coal. We used the OAP hall, which they gave free of charge. It was somewhere the men, their wives and the children too young to go to school could keep warm and have a hot meal. One day we had 400 people turn up."

'Mrs John said that the helpers used to cook the food at home and then take it down. "Maureen Morgan had four sons on strike and she used to make corned beef pie," she said. "We also had big cauldrons of cawl – anything we could get really."

'Mrs John recalls the Christmas of the strike. "We decided to hold a party for the kids and we went out collecting toys and made sure every child had a present. Santa Claus arrived on the Maesteg fire engine."

'Mrs John said one tot asked him for a bike. "He explained he could not manage it that year but maybe next time. It was heart-breaking. The little ones could not understand."'

The years 1984–85 was heart-breaking for so many in the south Wales Valleys.

Gyp and Violet were not directly involved in mining during that strike but both shared a deep sense of belonging to their community; both had a strong sense of justice and a commitment to those miners. It was those miners who sacrificed so much and then got short shrift from a government that destroyed them and their communities. It is the humanity, strength and kindness of people like Violet and Gyp that offers hope, the same cannot always be said for the callous actions of a cynical and uncaring Prime Minister.

It was not just in the Llynfi Valley where women became actively involved and significant social changes were emerging.

In the Cynon Valley and beyond it was the same, as Wendy Donovan wrote for the museum there in a blog post in 2014: 'During the 1980s the mining industry changed

Welshwomen defending their pits and communities.

for ever. Men and women left behind traditional roles and became politicised by the bitter clashes between the working classes and the Conservative government led by Margaret Thatcher, who branded the miners "the enemy within".'

Brenda Proctor (now sadly deceased) from the

North Staffordshire Miners' Wives Action Group in 1984 remembers, 'I said the strike wasn't about money but about communities and the future.' (*The Guardian*, 2014)

The 80s strike not only transformed the industrial landscape of Britain, it radically changed the lives of thousands of other women.

Brenda recalls how, early on in the strike (which started in March 1984), she was at a meeting in the local pit club where she expected a few other wives to volunteer support. 'But women turned up in droves wanting to help,' she says. 'It wasn't all about soup kitchens and food parcels – though that was important. We wanted to tell people why we were on strike.'

Within weeks the national Women Against Pit Closures campaign was launched. The women of miners' families were at the heart of the epic struggles against the Thatcher government. In March 1984, in Barnsley, 5,000 women from mining villages attended rallies and a few months later 23,000 marched through London. Women were arrested; they also chained themselves to colliery gates across the UK and Europe.

There was a great sense of solidarity.

However, it came at a cost as well, as some families were split by the trauma of the strike action and the pit closures.

The role of women has changed considerably during Gyp's lifetime. It's been argued that women have emerged out of the shadows with significant shifts in gender roles. The First and Second World Wars opened up factories and the world of work for women.

Women and children (under ten) were stopped from working down the pit in 1842 and, it could be argued, men should never have been continually working in such appalling conditions either. Post-pandemic, we are all accustomed to wearing face masks but there was only limited use of masks underground and the damaging coal dust was always being inhaled. The risk to life and limb was an ever-present fact of life. Women were always a part of that risk and that hardship, the role in the home was an extremely tough one.

The old tin baths by the fire was an enormous strain for families and for women in particular. It was a Rhondda woman, Elizabeth Andrews, who fought to set up pithead baths and this eased the relentless hardship of miners' wives lives filled by 'perpetual overwork, illness and suffering'.

Margaret Llewellyn Davies, Secretary of Women's Co-op Guild

Attitudes have changed and yet there are still remnants of that divide between the two sexes in some aspects of Valleys life. If there is a caring role it is statistically still more likely to be carried out by women, eighty per cent of all jobs in adult social care are done by women, and the proportion in direct care and support providing jobs is higher at eighty-five to ninety-five per cent.

On a more positive note, nearly half of the members of the Senedd are now women (forty-three per cent), which is considerable progress from a hundred years ago when women didn't even have the vote. Women are now visible in places where they previously weren't seen, in education, religion and politics.

Nobody would say the battle has been won and that the old gender hierarchy is no more, but there have been massive leaps forward. It could be argued that the demise of the old industrial landscape in south Wales has been a good thing for women, just as both the world wars served the cause of equality too.

In every discussion I've had with Gyp he has always acknowledged the incredible passion and strength women brought to bear in the battles to save the mining industry in south Wales. He knows how hard their lives were and how hard his mother worked to support her children and hold the family together. He has shed many tears in front of me as we have talked, and he has recalled those hardships endured by his mother. She was undoubtedly his rock and strength that has made him the heart-warming man he is now:

'You must remember that my mother was a true Christian and a Sunday school teacher. My father and I were not allowed to swear in the house or take the Lord's name in vain.

'The very first song I learned from my mother, when I could barely talk, was "Onward Christian Soldiers". You can imagine me and Dad worked in the pit where every other word was "fucking this" and "fucking that" and then having to go home at the end of a shift and not utter a single word of bad language. Because if I accidentally did swear I used to get a clodger off my mam.

'My mother had been a strong Christian woman all

Gyp with his children, sister and grandchildren on his wedding day in June 2024. As Gyp says: 'My family is my life, my bond, the reason I am who I am.'

Changing rooms of the pithead baths. Working miners from the 1970s in one (left), the other taken at Big Pit in 2022.

Publicity for the work of Caerau Men's Shed.

Leida's daughter and partner with Mr & Mrs Mayor.

Dai, Dai and Gyp, three lifelong friends.

The boys at Caerau Men's Shed.

Men's Shed calendar photos.

Men's Shed calendar photos.

Men's Shed choir.

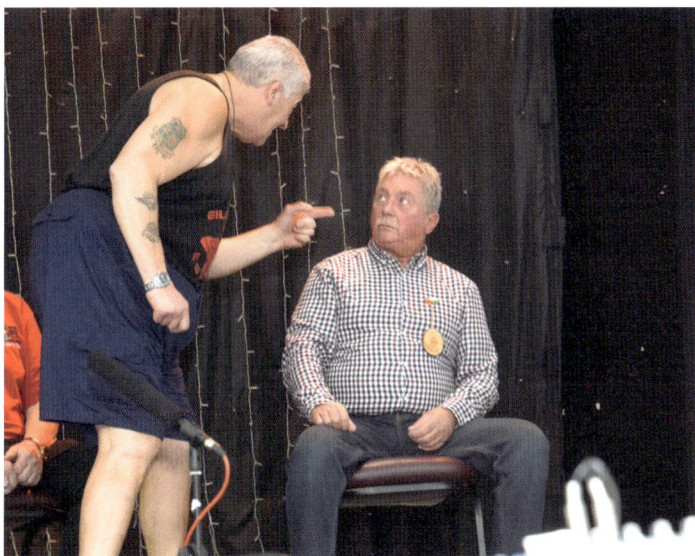

Men's Shed drama group and performance.

Gyp training at Billy's Gym.

Gyp giving a speech at his wedding, June 2024.

her life who was always helping others. She cared and supported those in real need. Mam used to wear a gold cross around her neck that me and my sister bought her. She loved it and never took it off.

'One day when I was visiting her in hospital she was diagnosed with cancer of the kidney. The doctor told us that Mam could live with one kidney but the next day we found out that Mam had been born with a deformed kidney and so it was not good enough to support her.

'Mam asked me, "Why? Why? I have been a good Christian all my life, so why has the Lord forsaken me now? Please answer me boy!"

'She ripped off her cross and threw it across the floor. I searched for that cross everywhere but I couldn't find it. I could not answer my mother's question, which bothered me. It kept me awake at nights after my mother passed away. Sometimes I still hear that question my mam asked.

'What is the answer? It still haunts me today, Churchy butty.'

I wish I had the answer for Gyp, but of course we all wonder why life can be so unfair and how difficult the issue of death is for all of us to cope with. These questions are almost a part of the human condition and we all struggle with them. Gyp's love for his mother and father is always so apparent in every conversation I have with him. It is clear they played such a vital role in making him the man he has become, the compassionate man, the caring man and even the wild man. I wish I could have met Mr and Mrs Davies.

For all of Gyp's own battles with drink and depression,

he has always supported his daughters and ensured they had opportunities to make their own way in life.

Gyp's battles also lead to him to find his own true love when he met Leida. They got married in 2024 and formally cemented their longstanding relationship. This book would not be complete without some words from her too, as she been integral to Gyp's life. Leida Salway, who became Leida Davies on 8th June 2024, wrote this for the book:

'His mother's death in 2003 hit him very hard, as they had always been very close. He lived in the next street to her in Nantyffyllon, in a house she had helped him buy, and he visited her every day, often more than once. He came from a close-knit mining family, with mammy at its heart, and they loved each other dearly. She was his greatest supporter, always going to watch him play, and was his shoulder to cry on when times were hard. Her death began his spiral into depression and he depended more and more on drinking to help cope with life.

'He had always led a full life, with plenty of male companions from his earliest times in the pit to playing as part of a team in both basketball and rugby but, as he got older and had to retire from sport, he still sought this companionship and found it by drinking with his mates. Always the joker, he was often the centre of attention which he enjoyed, even though he suffered for it the next day!

'Family problems, combined with changes at his workplace, added to this depression, as he found himself unable to cope without his beloved mother to help him. Taking early retirement from the paper mill left him

Gyp and Leida at their wedding in June 2024.

even more isolated from the male companionship he had always enjoyed and he sunk further into depression, resorting to staying in bed all morning, which led to him being unable to sleep at night and often having panic attacks when he went out.

'Not having achieved a lot academically at school, he lacked confidence in his own abilities and he needed someone to believe in him and encourage him to try to gain some qualifications. He had surprised everyone at the paper mill by, not only wanting to study for but in also gaining his NEBOSH (National Examination Board in Occupational Safety and Health) qualification. He then went on to study in Maesteg College for a qualification that enabled him to work in a school. This meant he could work once again with children (he had previously coached youth rugby) and this all helped him slowly out of the depressive state he had fallen into.

'Gradually he learned that he did not need the crutch

he found in drink, a crutch that he had relied on so heavily. With encouragement, he joined the Maesteg Gleemen Choir, giving him the male companionship he had missed. At the same time his involvement with Caerau Men's Shed gave him not only companionship but a purpose to his life as he realised many men had suffered in the same way as himself. He later went on to form the Llynfi Valley Ex-Miners' Group which brought him back full circle to spend some time with men he knew from his early days in the coal mines.

'My role throughout the last twenty years has been to support and encourage him and provide him with the unconditional love that he lost when his mother died.'

I've known him since I was nineteen through rugby. In his twenties he sang 'If I was a rich man' completely naked in the car park. Then he got thirty other men to do it with him… all stark naked. One of those naked players was getting picked up by his new girlfriend's parents, and he got in their car still naked. Gyp was well known for singing it. It happened more than once. It was almost like his theme tune and he was always naked too.
Darren Williams @Caerau Men's Shed

Like father like son and the dreaded drink

FIGURES FOR THE UK suggest that around three million children grow up in single-parent households and ninety per cent of those households are single mums.

Christopher Davies did not come from a single-parent household and neither did his children. Gyp's parents stayed together but it was a bumpy road at times and some of the memories are painful ones. His father's drinking posed many problems for the family, and he struggled to get a real handle on it. The rows in the house were often really bad.

Gyp remembers when his mother hit his father on the head with a poker from the fireplace and the blood was on the walls. Gyp remembers running out of the house in his pyjamas in bare feet and it was snowing. He ran and ran and didn't know where he was going, but he just wanted to get away.

It wasn't all bad though and it's a love story that endured through the war years and through the struggles of life in the Valleys. The family has a box of letters exchanged between Gyp's mother Doris and his father Danny during the war.

In 1939 Danny was stationed in Brize Norton before going overseas, and Doris was working as a housekeeper/maid for a rich lady in Golders Green in London.

Their relationship obviously had stresses and strains during this time, as Danny writes this to Doris: 'I admit I am bad sometimes but not all the time I acted decent to you and you cannot say different. I have written bad letters to you and you have done the same to me. Well Doris there's one thing I hope you don't do, and that is to play and act decent towards Frank because he would be just the boy to suit you, but all the time he would be with you I shall be grinding my teeth at the thought that you might one day have been my wife because I loved you Doris and always will. Well I have lost you and I did break my heart over it because it was no joke for anybody to laugh at, perhaps you will have a good laugh but it will only be your ignorance.

'Yes I have found a girl, you said I would find a girl and I have settled down to her. I was with her parents last Sunday for tea and they were charming people and she is a nice girl too. I guess she is too good for me but I have told her what I have been and she knew it before I met her, but I have promised her I shall never drink so long as I have got her to think about, and I got seven days for being drunk and disorderly up in Warmwell for breaking that window and they sure hit the stuffing out of me and I thought I was tough. So it has taught me a lesson about what the price of beer is. Well I shall say this before I finish:

'I still love you and always will because you are the only one I really loved and, although I have got a girl now, I am the broken-hearted clown. I hope you don't mind if I give you this one kiss X and seal it tight for my sake.

'PS: Please don't tell anybody about me having seven days because it would break my mother's heart.'

Sometime later, when things had perhaps been somewhat repaired between Danny and Doris, there is a letter from Danny's mother to Doris that says:

'Dear Doris, Many thanks for your letter, very pleased to hear from you and I hope the raids are not too bad there now. We have had a couple of quiet nights here. I have just received a letter from Danny, He is so proud, as you were, that he has been promoted to a corporal. He is coming on fine and I have told him he must look after himself and keep off the beer.

'He receives good money now. Of course there are always some who don't like to see others get on. But many have told me he is a smart boy, and if he will keep off the beer I am sure you would not wish for a better lad. He has never brought trouble to me in any way and I am his mother and I know for certain if you will stick to him you will make a man of him. He really worships you and he always has from your school days, he has often confided in me that you are the only girl for him...'

Danny's battles with the dreaded beer seem to predate his worst war experiences and he writes to Doris too confirming their obvious bond, but also alludes to the trials of separation and the obvious issues Danny has managing his drinking. It is easy to forget that they are both still teenagers at this time and, with the long lens of the twenty-first century, we recognise that adulthood is not an instant given when you just happen to turn eighteen.

Danny wrote the following letter (Gyp believes someone

wrote it on his father's behalf because his writing skills were limited) from Brize Norton in Oxfordshire in 1939:

'Dear Doris, I am now going to explain and tell you the reasons for all that I have done to you, and after I have wrote this letter to you Darling, I hope you will forgive me, please Doris because I love you too much to give it all up. Darling, try and forgive me the way I have made a beast of myself towards you, you know very well I only tried to make you jealous by writing to Olive. The reason why I wrote to Olive is I was in such a panic and did not know what to do, so by writing to Olive I thought that was the only way to get you back, because I keep telling you, for the last time, I love you and won't give you up never, so please, I am begging for you to forgive me. Darling, if I have hurt you bad as I know I have, there must be a little bit of love for me because I have got it bad for you and I am telling you the truth, may God strike me dead as I am writing to you. So please try and pass it off, Darling, and tell Olive I am deeply sorry to her for what I have done between her and David. I must have been out of my head to write to Olive when I introduced David to her so tell her, I am very sorry what I have done to her.'

Danny then writes to her in September 1940 when the couple are obviously trying to get married. He writes:

'My own darling Doris. Just these few lines my sweetheart, hoping to find you quite safe because those air raids and the damage they are causing up there make me worried so much. I hope that you're quite well my Darling, and the old Lady.

'I received a letter from my mother on Saturday and she said that your father wouldn't give his consent. I don't know what he has against me, if it is the beer I suppose.

'But Dearest, I would give my life to make you happy because I love you too much for me to make you unhappy but I guess he wouldn't understand how we feel about each other.

'I think it is mean for anyone to stop anybody from getting married, especially when they are so much in love.

'Well Dearest, I feel so miserable and unhappy I could cry my eyes out because I had my heart so set on getting married at the end of the month. You said you hadn't heard from your father. I hoped to God and prayed every night that he would say yes for his consent for us to get married sweetheart.

'Well Darling, if he has refused we shall have to wait until you're 21 because I shall never give you up my sweetheart if I will have to wait all my life, because you're everything to me.

'My mother said that, from the top to the bottom of the street, everybody knows about us getting married. So how they know I couldn't tell you sweetheart, but I honestly swear it to God that I told my mother not to tell a single person about it until we had got married, so you can see how news goes about.'

Their relationship, as the letters illustrate, endured from their formative teenage years right through to old age. They grappled with war, separation, hardship and trauma. Their love matured and grew over many, many years.

Gyp in full swing for the Men's Shed calendar!

Gyp's abiding memory of his mam and dad is of their love for each other and their children. They married during the war and his mother's wedding dress was made out of parachute silk.

But even their wedding day had high drama. The Germans dropped a mine and it landed in the tree outside the church, so they all had to spend the wedding night there inside, until the bomb disposal unit arrived the next day.

Danny and Doris became parents in the days when children played out for long periods and were just left to get on with it, without any real adult supervision. Those days when you could disappear for hours with a bottle of council pop (water!) and a couple of jam sandwiches. The days when children walked to school, just like the miners who often walked two miles to work come rain or shine. Both the children and the adults were accustomed to being hardy and resourceful. It was the time when children were often seen and not heard, and yet that very nearly cost Gyp his life when he was playing out one day.

He recalls the day when everything could so easily have come to a very abrupt and tragic end when he was still a child: 'When I was young there was a tree that had a rope swing on it that swung out right over the river and back. Me and the boys spent hours there, it was at the bottom of Kings Terrace in Nantyffyllon.

'I must have been about ten or eleven years old when a gang of older boys grabbed hold of me and tied me to the tree. They wound the long rope around and around my body. What they didn't know, when they left me there, was that the rope was around my neck. I was too high off the ground for my butties to help me and I began to choke and lose consciousness.

'I blacked out and the next thing I remember was my father carrying me home in his arms. The boys had run about a mile to fetch my father to rescue me. I am sure if he wasn't available or the boys had left it any longer I would be dead.

'Still brings shivers to me today.'

How life can turn on a sixpence! Credi's predictions for young Christopher Davies would have been short-lived. Gyp's father went to see the families of the lads who'd bullied his son, and I'm sure those boys became only too aware of what the consequences of their actions might have been. Their lives would have turned out very differently then too.

Gyp's stories of his childhood give an insight into the many sides of the man who now offers so much to everyone in his community. He is a man who wants opportunities for all.

That brutal story of bullies who nearly caused a very real tragedy is balanced out by the heart-warming story he told me of how he rescued a boy off the school roof when he was ten years old. I can completely believe the kind and assertive manner of young Gyp, who even had the maturity to very rightly chide the teacher for his limited approach to the real struggles some children faced.

Gyp tells it like this: 'There was a class that would have been called special needs back then, and they had loads of comics like the *Beano* and the *Dandy*. In those times they had a coal fire in the classroom and one day the comics caught light. The fire was put out quite quickly but one boy was going to get the blame, so he ran off. He climbed onto the school roof and hid in the old bell tower.

The teachers tried to coax him down but he wouldn't budge. A large crowd of pupils and teachers gathered as he wasn't shifting.

'The teachers knew I could climb because the week before I'd gone on to the roof to fetch our rugby ball. I had the cane for climbing up there then.

'But word went round and the teacher says, "Right, Davies, get up there and bring him down."

'"But I had the cane for going up there last week sir?" I said.

'"Don't be cheeky, lad," said the teacher. "Just get up there."

'I climbed up the drainpipe and scrambled up the slates to the bell tower. It started pissing down.

'Right enough, the boy was there, shivering in amongst the pigeon shit. He knew me as I'd befriended him before and I'd looked out for him.

'"Come on down, butty boy," I said.

'"No," he said, "I'm afraid and I'm starving."

'"Right," I said. "If I go and get you a box of Potato Puffs, will you come down then?" I knew they were his favourite.

'"Yes," he said, "But all the children will have to go."

'So I climb down again and get soaked to the skin.

'"Well?" said Mr Williams, the head teacher, "what did he say?"

'"He's soaking, cold and starving sir," I said. "He wants the children to go in and I promised to take him a box of Potato Puffs. Then he'll come down."

'So I went off to get the crisps and then returned to the drainpipe. But then I realised I needed both hands to climb so I couldn't carry the crisps up.

'"I can't do it, sir," I said and told him why.

'"Is anyone willing to help Davies?" asked the Head. Not one person put their hand up.

'"Fuck this!" I said.

'"What did you say, Davies?" asked the Head, looking ominous.

'"I said it's bad luck this, sir. I'll have to go up without the crisps."

'So up I went again and I said to the boy, "Look, I've got you a box of Potato Puffs but I couldn't fetch them up to you because I needed both hands to climb."

'"It's OK," said the lad. "I can come down with you and help you carry them up."

'I thought, "He is fucking nuts," but I played along with it and made sure he went down first so he wouldn't run back up.

'On the way down the whole school was chanting "Gyp! Gyp! Gyp!"

'When we got to the bottom the teacher grabbed the boy by the scruff of the neck and was going to wallop him. I grabbed the teacher's arm before he could hit him and said, "Perhaps that's why he hid up there in the first place, sir?"

'He let him go and we were allowed to eat the Potato Puffs. We ate them in the shelter, the whole box, all thirty bags of them with big smiles on our faces, soaking wet and cold but happy.

'Even at that age I was trying my best to help people.'

That story really sums up so much about Gyp, his sense of fairness and his tremendous empathy for his fellow humans. It demonstrates his simple and straightforward way of telling it how it is and shows how he will always go that extra mile for someone else.

Those times were different, teachers would give you a 'clip round the ear' and money was always tight and nobody had anything, but it meant everyone was poor so they really were all in it together.

The pressures on families in those days, when people counted every penny, were in many ways quite extreme. The mitigating factor in the Valleys was the sense of community that was so strong and the support networks ran deep. If someone didn't show their face one day someone would always knock the door and check they were OK.

The troubles families faced inside those four walls were often very intense and the culture of male drinking was strong. Nowadays, the young face other pressures with social media and the Valleys being awash with all manner of drugs.

Gyp's sister witnessed far more than him because it was felt that their dad mellowed with age. As a younger man, Gyp's sister saw it all and would often talk to him and make it quite clear their father wasn't quite the hero Gyp thought he was. Gyp couldn't handle that vision of his hero, his old man. He was in denial of the full picture of family life until he was much older and he put the pieces of the jigsaw together.

But of course, Danny Davies's life was not a simple one, he had suffered significant trauma in the war and worked most of his life in such a tough trade as mining. Hard lives and hard drinking often went hand in hand. Perhaps the really tough men were the teetotallers... just a thought!

The patterns in families are not lost on Gyp. He nearly blew his own life through drink and was wayward and wild for many years. He got married far too young and his young man's appetite for the party and nightclub lifestyle was partly stolen away from him. Gyp's ex-wife might well say he claimed his youth back by going out and getting drunk regardless of his family responsibilities. He acknowledges that his drinking and living life to excess was what ultimately destroyed his marriage and it upsets him because the responsibility lies solely with him and that fills him with remorse about bad decisions he made.

As Gyp himself says: 'There were times when I couldn't walk home from the club because I was so drunk. So I used to phone my eldest daughter, who was a teenager then, to come up and she'd help me home. When I'd get home I used to pay the girls fifty pence each to take my shoes off because I was so drunk I couldn't undo my laces.

'There'd be other times then when they'd bring boyfriends home and I'd be in bed after drinking, and of course our toilet was downstairs, so I'd walk through the living room bollock naked to go to the toilet. That was embarrassing for them.

'They put up with me.

'My ex-wife was working and as soon as she went out to work I'd be up the club straightaway to have a drink, and I'd pay my girls money to say I hadn't been out. I'd come home just before my ex-wife got back from work.

'I used to bribe the girls which was not right, but that's when the drink had me.'

Gyp's self-destructive behaviours at this time really threw his life into turmoil. He is open and brutally honest about his pain and the suffering it caused to those he held dear around him. He described that period of his life to me like this:

'My marriage was suffering because of my behaviour, which ultimately resulted in the pain of divorce. My mother died which really affected me. My father also died. It was a mixture of events; I was really fucked up mentally, butty.

'You can't imagine what it was like; my head was like a cement mixer. I just couldn't cope. At this time my weight went up to 26 stone which also added to all my problems.

'I nearly lost my job in the paper mill for coming to work drunk.'

There was no lasting damage to Gyp's daughters or any hangover of blame regarding the parenting they had though. In fact, quite the opposite. His eldest daughter was so proud that her father's story was appearing in a book that, when he asked her, she was keen to contribute this:

'What was it like having me as a father? "Just write a few words," my father said.

'It was the "few words" that was the hard part because as soon as he asked if I would like to contribute to the book, it opened a floodgate of memories and anecdotes that swirled around my mind for days.

'But I couldn't capture them to put them onto paper.

'Obviously, bias is going to be a problem for, what is your father if he is not your hero?

'Also, how can I share what I believe is the essence of my father if I don't quite understand it myself? However, as my father has always been a believer in giving things a go, here we go!

'My father has something special. He is kind, caring, understanding, and funny – all the qualities that are found to be so endearing to others. But there is something more. To simplify things, we could say he is a "people person" but this does not describe the way in which people are drawn to him. Not only are they drawn to him, but they also remember him (although this might be in part down to his rugby player stature and cauliflower ears!). He is warm and welcoming. He listens and he is interested. He is funny and self-deprecating. He tells it like it is, but he is fair and he genuinely wants to help others; although it is the needs of others that drives him on.

'My parents were teenagers when I arrived. They were newly-married (partly by necessity!) and lived with my grandparents at first.

'I like to imagine the way they met was like a scene from *Romeo and Juliet* (but I am an English teacher!). My father remembers the weather was warm, the sun in the sky, and he was working near Coegnant pit. My mother walked past with her long hair shining in the sun, licking an ice-cream, and my father called out for her to share it with him. The rest, as they say, is history.

'I can only imagine how difficult it must have been being such young parents (just seventeen and eighteen years old) and it wasn't all plain sailing, but my childhood was full of long summers traipsing the mountains, happy school days and a close-knit family. I loved my home and was always intensely homesick whenever I was away from it.

'Growing up, I began to understand that my father was legendary in rugby circles. I think this may have had something to do with his fearless and feisty action on the field in comparison with his warmth and humour in the clubhouse after. His legendary status could be a bit limiting at times though, and I was beginning to think that I would never get a boyfriend with the warning that came with courting "Gyp's Daughter".

'On the up side, I was never, ever short of rugby players from Nantyffyllon RFC offering to walk me home safely, such was the respect they had for my father. My father only had two rules as far as boyfriends were concerned – no footballers and no Maesteg Celtic rugby players! I'm afraid I broke both these rules, but only briefly, as your father is always right in the end!

'My father's infamy was worldwide. I remember talking to a friend of mine who had recently been to Australia with Welsh Rugby. He told me had gone back to the clubhouse after the game and was chatting to a local Aussie. The conversation went something like this:

'Aussie: Where are you from in Wales?

'Taffy: Near Cardiff.

'Aussie: I know Cardiff – where exactly?

'Taffy: Somewhere called Bridgend.

'Aussie: I know that area – where in Bridgend?

'Taffy: A little village called Maesteg.

'Aussie: I know Maesteg. Hey – do you know Gyp?

'My rugby-playing friend said he flew to the other side of the world, played his first game in Australia, only to go back to the clubhouse to speak to someone whose first question was, "Do you know Gyp?"

'Like I said, he is a legend.

'My father always saw the fun in things. The few times that he would be left in charge of making our tea after school he would pretend that we were in a restaurant and serve us like a waiter, folding the kitchen paper in a triangle like a serviette. He was beyond pleased with himself when he learnt how to use the pressure cooker and made corn beef stew for the first time. He supported us in all that we did. When he took me to gymnastics at the girls' school once, he was reported for being a prowler as he wandered about the building, killing time while I trained. This still makes me laugh.

'He was once mistaken for the undertaker as he accompanied me to my boyfriend's grandfather's wake, holding a wreath in his hand. He was directed to the coffin – then he explained who he was (I'm smiling at this memory too!).

'We once drove all the way to Brecon to get a new ribbon for his grandfather's Zulu War medal from the Brecon Royal Welsh Regimental Museum. We sang to Roy Orbison songs as we drove over the mountains. They offered quite a bit of money for that Zulu War medal but my father refused – he is so intensely proud of his heritage. These are just a few anecdotes and memories – really, I could write a book, but someone else beat me to it!

'I hope this has given a little insight into what it was like having "Gyp" for my father. As time has gone on, I have had to get used to sharing my father as he means so many things to so many different people. To me he will always be Dad – someone who unconditionally, and for eternity, will always have my back – and I am so very proud of him, and slightly jealous that someone is writing a book about him!'

As his daughter says, her mother and father got married when he was only eighteen and his wife was younger at seventeen. They married because she was pregnant and they thought they were doing the right thing and the decent thing. They remained married for over thirty years and, even after divorcing, they remained close until her recent death.

Gyp's youngest daughter also wanted to contribute to the book and sent this to me through her father:

'As far back as I can remember my father ALWAYS had time for me, although he had a busy life working twelve-hour shifts at the mill and, of course, his love of rugby meant he was often playing at weekends. He is funny, caring, loving and compassionate. He has always been a hardworking man.

'I love him... he is my hero and my rock through stormy waters.'

This story has talked about Gyp and his relationships with so many different individuals and groups, from the mines to the Men's Shed. His two daughters call him their hero and it was the same for Gyp with his father Daniel. Their relationship runs through this story as does the relationship between Gyp and his mother. His father did thirty-five years in the pit before he took a job in the paper mill when he was older – those years when he was no longer quite so wild. It might be that the much easier workload of the paper mill played its part in mellowing Daniel Davies.

Gyp has reflected on that relationship with his father and reflected on the toll that the hard drinking took on both their lives: 'We must remember that when I went to work down the pit in 1970 I didn't have to go and work there because there were loads of jobs around at that time. I went down the pit because I wanted to be like my father who I thought was a real man.

'He was tough, unassuming, macho, like a film star

and a war hero all in one. He was everything you really wanted a man to be. I wanted to be a model of him.

'I knew he drank but when I was young I thought that's what real men did... but I was wrong. In my younger days I myself drank and nearly lost my job and my marriage because of it.

'I'm writing this down for you now because I need people to see how a drinking culture can so easily take a hold of you.

'I was really bad at one stage of my life.'

Although Gyp's dad was a big drinker he had hard rules for his son. He didn't want to see him drinking or smoking as a young teenager. As time went on they would often get drunk together, but that was when Gyp had grown up.

As Gyp says: 'If my dad saw me put a fag in my mouth or take a swig of alcohol he'd give me a clout. He caught me smoking once when I was seventeen and just out of a colliery shift. He walked in and saw me with a fag in my mouth and he smacked me in the gob, "Don't let me catch you smoking again," he said.

'As I got older we used to arm wrestle in the pub, me and me dad. And when I was older I was beating him one day and he smacked me in the mouth and knocked my tooth out. We were drunk though, so I didn't feel it. It was what we did, we had this macho rivalry.'

As Gyp has got older he has been able to gain a bit of perspective on many things about his life. He has thought a lot about the struggles and difficulties his mother and father both faced in their lives. Times were hard and they both faced their own personal demons. They both

Gyp with his daughters.

needed medical help at certain points for depression and the extreme pressures that pushed them to the very edge at times.

Gyp has a memory as a young boy of accompanying his mother to one of her ECT treatments. He looked

103

Gyp looking smart to meet Santa!

through the glass and saw it taking place and it was not something a young boy should have witnessed.

Electroconvulsive treatment is still used today but evokes some strong opinions and lingering memories of the film *One Flew Over the Cuckoo's Nest*. Some doctors claim it has good results for people experiencing severe depression but they can't account for exactly why it works. From Gyp's point of view, he believes it affected his mother's memory.

Research suggests about seventy per cent of those treated with ECT are women. This might be because depression is more likely to be diagnosed in women, but it does open up a real can of worms about gender and mental health... and we're back to that question of what makes a man (or a woman?).

The context of Gyp's life does help to understand some of his wild behaviours, as he says himself: 'I've done loads of stuff I'm ashamed of. I've even pinched lead off a disused church roof. I'm not proud of it. When you look back you know it was wrong but it was what we all did. We found out how we could get money from lead and copper wire.

'There were a lot of abandoned houses with old wooden sash windows with lead counterweights. So we stripped them down after one of the boy's fathers had told us we could make money from them. We got lead from everywhere then. We stripped a derelict farm roof. It was always abandoned places, not places where people lived.

'We also took electric cables from some run-down cottages. We used pinchers and hammers to get to the copper wire. But, unknown to me, one of the fucking wires was still live. I put the metal pinchers on the cable and banged it hard with the hammer. There was a big blue flash and I ended up lying on my back in the middle of the road. I'd travelled some way and the boys were all pissing themselves.'

Gyp's life is this wonderful mixture of laughter and tears (it could be argued everyone's life is, but Gyp seems to have these wonderful extreme stories that are never far away from each other). The pain is there as plain as day as he grew into the tough world of colliers and coal. He was born into a part of Britain that was forged by heavy industry and the rules of survival sometimes bore harsh consequences, but there was always something to laugh about and that very unique sense of belonging and community.

He's a fucking idiot!

Actually he's a really conscientious and caring person. If help is needed he'd be the first one to put his hand up…

but if you fell on the floor playing rugby don't expect to get up 'cos he'll kick the shit out of you.

And I love him 'cos he's like my cuz.

Sam Leach @Caerau Men's Shed

A sporting life

Sport has played a significant role in Gyp's life and gave him an outlet for all that childhood energy.

You always have to remember that he was almost born in a rugby stand, as his mother's waters broke while she was watching a Maesteg match in 1955! Gyp didn't find rugby – it found him. His parents' ashes are spread over the rugby field at Nantyffyllon.

He did not find school easy. Even in primary school he was sent out of lessons for poor behaviour, but sport was an area where he excelled and found a sense of purpose and achievement. In fact, the teachers often gave Gyp little jobs and errands to keep him quiet and to keep him in order. So he'd be off rubbing dubbin into rugby balls and putting linseed oil on cricket bats… the lengths teachers went to making sure Gyp survived school!

The first real rugby match that Gyp remembers was when he was nine years old. He was playing at the Old Nanty rugby field (a recycling plant these days) for Nantyffyllon Primary School against Garth Primary.

He was unaware that his mother was sat on the mountainside watching him!

The ball shot out of a boy's arms and up into the air. Gyp collected the spilled ball and, in his excitement, started to speed towards the try line, the rest of his team left behind shouting his name. The try line beckoned towards him with not another player in sight and over Gyp went to score a try and make a name for himself!

He was so proud to score his first-ever try. The teacher and the rest of his team were waiting for him at the halfway line!

'Oh Davies,' the teacher said, 'what a scorching run. I've only got one little suggestion to make – could you please run towards the opposition try line next time please?'

Gyp had run the wrong way and to his dismay his mother had seen it all. And she never let him forget it!

When he got to comprehensive school he excelled at sport and went on to play basketball for Wales and played rugby for various senior clubs and represented the Boys' Club of Wales.

Sports teacher Brian Sparks was an important person who looked out for Gyp and saw his potential, but he was certainly no soft touch. Gyp recalls one occasion when he forgot his kit and Mr Sparks sent him and another boy up to the classroom to write out the Lord's Prayer ten times. Neither boy could remember the last few lines so they wrote it out ten times with each one incomplete. When they presented their

Brian Sparks, Gyp's PE teacher.

work to Mr Sparks he looked at it with disdain and said: 'This simply isn't good enough, boys!'

Both boys were then ordered to bend over and get hit by the dap. Gyp was hit so hard that, when he visited the toilets, it hurt so much he called other lads in to see the damage. They told him the Dunlop logo was visible on his bare backside. There was then a queue of boys outside the toilet to view the Dunlop logo on Gyp's bottom.

But he never forgot his gym kit again!

Now Gyp's grandsons have both been capped at Under-19 level by Wales and so the sporting tradition goes on.

Gyp still lifts weights and visits Billy's Gym where he's been going on and off for forty-four years. When Gyp was struggling with depression he found the gym a safe and positive place.

He says: 'Boxing kept my mind focused and I always felt good after a session with the heavy punch bag. The weight training would stop me from being lethargic and pump the blood to my heart and brain. I would have a moment of peace and calm after a hard gym session.'

He went on to say: 'Your body is full of muscles, use them or lose them… and anyway I have my reputation to keep up, LOL.'

Gyp's reputation wasn't always a positive one as he recalls: 'One match I broke a player's jaw and they must have complained to the committee of my club because on the following training night I was called in to a meeting of the committee and told that I would have to curb my aggressive behaviour. They said I was too rough.

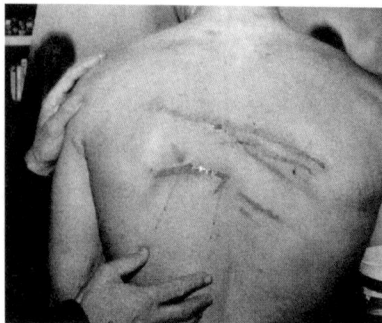

Gyp's back, with the battle scars from the rugby field.

'"Yes, I might be too rough," I said and then I lifted up my shirt and showed them the stud marks running down my back. "I get marks like these every match, gentlemen." Then I walked out of the room and not another word was said about it. I got knocked unconscious and I got punched, it was the law of the jungle on the rugby field in the 1970s.'

Gyp's mother and father were massive supporters of his during his rugby playing days and were there on the touchline. His mam was so proud of him.

He remembers: 'There was one match when my butty broke his leg and they carried him off in a large blanket because the club didn't have a stretcher. My mam was furious about that. She told the committee there was no way her boy would ever be carried off a pitch in a blanket. So she went around the touchline collecting money until she had enough to buy a stretcher for the club. Luckily I never had to use it but there were plenty that did.'

That 'reputation' is also a mixed bag when it comes to the dreaded drink.

The drinking culture has blighted many lives from Boris Yeltsin to Gazza, but it always offers a host of stories and anecdotes, like Andy Powell driving a golf buggy down the M4.

Those drinking anecdotes often carry a darker side

Cartoon versions of Gyp's rugby days, one highlighting his many red cards and the other capturing him in full flow.

where innocent bystanders or family members are not considered during bouts of drunken and anti-social behaviour. Just like the violence of the times, the drinking culture was an inherent part of the rugby club back then.

The stories can be enjoyed but they must be placed in context. If sixty-year-old men are still getting blind drunk and wetting themselves in police cells, is that still so amusing?

Gyp has a mine of stories, some more palatable than others.

There was the time he went on a rugby trip to Twickenham to watch the England v Wales game. After the game they were all very drunk.

All the boys needed the loo and climbed up a bank and were stood in a row peeing. They called to Gyp, who was down below keeping a watch for any policemen, to come up and see something terrible.

Gyp scaled the bank and saw the other side was overlooking a sewage treatment plant. In the middle of the works was a swan caught in one of the arms that was slowly sweeping round the sewage in a circle.

'Save it Gyp!' the boys implored him. So he jumped in and waded through the awful stink and sludge until he reached the swan. It was only then that he discovered it wasn't a real one, it was a plastic swan.

They then went for a Chinese meal but the restaurant wouldn't let Gyp in because of the state he was in and the smell coming from him. He had to stay outside and watch the rest of them eat their meal through the window.

There was another occasion when he was on tour to

Brixham in Devon and, late one night, he and a few others decided to try and steal a trawler. Gyp had climbed up to the crow's nest to look out, when a panda car pulled up with blue lights flashing. A big Devon copper gave them a choice of either meeting the trawlermen whose boat they were trying to steal or being arrested and taken to the police station. They chose the arrest as they figured the trawlermen would be a step too far for a few drunken Valleys boys.

Somewhat ironically, Gyp did make friends with a trawlerman following another tour to Brixham. He played against a man by the name of Frank Worthington, and they became friends and he has been back to visit him. Gyp split his ear in half during a game and his wife then attacked him with her handbag when he came off the field.

Gyp says of him: 'The last time I went to see him he was out on a trawler, so I left a message for him at the rugby club. He was older than me but hard as fuck. He was a legend in Brixham. I got sent off for punching him in the lughole but I had the worst end of the stick when his missus hit me with her handbag full of change she'd been collecting for the raffle.'

I'll just give you one more story of another rugby scrape. This time it was a trip to Edinburgh in the 1970s for Scotland v Wales. Everyone watched the game and got much worse for wear afterwards.

Gyp, ever the gentleman, offered to walk a woman to the station for her train, and on the way he suggested they took a photo to remember the day. They noticed someone in the photo booth, so they left it. On the return journey, half an hour later, Gyp noticed the same person's legs were still sat in the photo booth, so he pulled back the curtain and discovered a Welsh boy very drunk – he'd passed out. Gyp called over to a few other Welsh lads who were nearby to give him a hand.

He said to the others, men he'd never met before: 'We can't leave him here boys, it's too dangerous. My bus leaves at midnight, let's get him to my bus meeting point and we'll take him home to Wales and sort it out there.'

When they got to Gyp's bus, his own boys said, 'Who the fuck is that, Gyp?'

'I don't fucking know,' said Gyp. 'But we can't leave him here, he's Welsh, mun. Let's put him on the back seat and let him sleep it off and we can keep an eye on him.'

The other boys agreed, with the condition that if he spewed or wet himself, it was on Gyp to clean it up.

When they got to Wales he was still out of it. 'Where you going to take him?' the boys asked Gyp.

They searched his pockets and found an old betting slip with an address on the back in Ogmore Vale.

So eventually they pull up at the address and it takes three of them to carry him off the bus because he's still out of it.

A lady opened the door and Gyp said, 'I may be wrong, but is this yours?'

'Yes,' said the lady, 'It's my son but what's he doing here?'

'We brought him home,' said Gyp.

'Home!' she said, 'But he's supposed to be on his honeymoon in Scotland.'

They laid the boy on the couch and made a hasty retreat back to the bus. They laughed on their way home but, as Gyp says, 'God knows what his new wife was thinking. There were no mobile phones back in those days and we never found out what happened to them.'

Gyp and I have had lengthy discussions about the drinking culture that exists in Britain. It is perceived by some as yobbish and anti-social. Are we any worse than our European neighbours? That is a topic that requires a lot more research and debate than we are able to give it in these pages.

There certainly seems to be a rites of passage element involved in everyone's lives, and young people have to navigate their way through it without suffering any lasting damage – or they could take that teetotal route and avoid the potentially toxic drink and drugs culture. Whatever way you look at it, young people have to make a working relationship with drugs and alcohol. They have to ensure they don't get knocked off track and that they don't fall in love with substances and end up on the hard road of addictions.

Those teenage

Gyp performing for the Men's Shed calendar!

and early twenties years are such a tough time to grapple with, and youngsters are at that age where they least want to listen to boring adults droning on and giving them lectures. You have to hope enough good, solid stuff went into them early on to ensure they can come through unscathed.

The day
Gyp met The King

AFTER MANY MEETINGS and emails and social media messages, I thought we had it all nailed down and Gyp's story was complete. Then he sends me an email just before the start of the Six Nations. He told me it was prompted by a documentary programme retelling the story of the famous Welsh sides of the 1970s. He'd completely forgotten his brush with royalty and thought I might like the story of it for the book.

Now when he mentioned royalty I got a bit worried, I just couldn't see him going on bended knee to anyone and doffing his cap and felt it might radically change my image of him as a real champion of us ordinary people. It didn't!

Here's what he sent me: 'Churchy, I forgot this story until I watched the programme *Slammed* on TV about Welsh rugby in the 1970s.

'I was invited to the Marriott Hotel in Cardiff around 2003 to receive my silver medal for services to the paper-making union the GPMU. I had a great night, got drunk and missed the last train home, so I decided to try and book a hotel in Cardiff. I managed to get into the Jury Hotel and booked over the phone using my bank card.

'I found my way to the hotel around 11pm. I went

The award Gyp received for his trade unionism in keeping the workplace accident free.

straight to the reception desk and the person said, "Good evening sir, what can I do for you?"

'I said, "It's Mr Davies, I booked a room for the night by card over the phone."

'He replied, "I'm sorry sir, there's nothing here?"

'I said, "I phoned about an hour ago and the person took my card details and booked a room for me."

'"I'm sorry sir, we've got nothing here."

'"Well can I book a room now?"

'"No, I'm sorry sir, we're full."

'I began to raise my voice, "You fucking useless twats, I'm from the Valleys and the last train has gone!"

'"Why don't you try a hostel, sir?"

'"Fuck a hostel, I'm in no state to go wandering around Cardiff this time of the night."

'"There's no need to raise your voice, sir," he said.

'I said, "Listen boyo, I am pissed and I'm tired and I'm far from home."

'At that moment a voice from behind me said, "What's the matter, bach?"

'I turned around ready to say "and you can fuck off" when I recognised it was "The King", Barry John.

'"Look," he said, "do you see that table over there with an empty pint glass on it? Go and sit there and I will see what I can do."

'"OK butty," I replied. I was thinking, "Fucking hell it's The King... The King!"

'He returned to the table after a while with a key for a room. I couldn't thank him enough. By now it was about 12 o'clock so I said, "Let me buy you a pint, Barry."

'"OK bach," he said. "That would be nice."

'So off I went to get The King a pint and one for myself and returned to the table. There was only me and Barry in the lounge. I asked him what he was doing there and he said he'd been on one of those sports forums and had a bit too much to drink, so he'd booked a room for the night.

'He asked me where I was from and what my name was. I told him my name and he said that he knew Chico Hopkins from Maesteg and stated how good the Maesteg pack of forwards were in the 1970s. I said that I played rugby and told him my nickname was Gyp.

'He said, "I've heard about you in rugby circles. I believe you're a bit of a header on the field, bach, aren't you?"

'More beer was consumed. I think I made a mistake and asked him why he had retired from rugby at 26 years of age when he was such a legend.

'I said, "Barry, my mother loved you when you were playing for Wales. She used to shout at the TV: 'Come on my boy.'"

'"Go on, phone her," he said, "Tell her who you're with, mun, go on, do it!"

Gyp with Barry John (The King) and the badges Barry John sent to Gyp after they met.

'"Barry," I said. "It's now 2am, she'll be in bed, mun!"

'"Go on, go on!" he said.

'So I phoned my mam but there was no answer; I knew that would happen.

'Barry seemed disappointed. "Let's have more beer, bach," he said.

'"Aye, go on then, butty," I said.

'He came back with more pints.

'"It's OK like this see, bach," he said. "But back then in the '70s I couldn't go outside the door to take my bloody dog for a walk without the press hounding me you see, boyo."

'"But you're a legend, butty!" I said.

'Then he said, "I never wanted to be a King or a legend, I'm just a boy who loved to play rugby and express my skills. Rugby was the game that let me express those skills. I used to love going away to Spain on holidays with my family because no one knew who I was out there. I had peace for a while see, bach."

'At this stage I looked at the clock, it was 3 30am.

'"Let's have another beer over at the bar, Gyp," he said.

'"OK," I said.

'He talked more about rugby and the game. He told me he had opened a Chinese restaurant called BJ's in Cardiff and invited me there when I was available. I loved all the stories about him playing rugby for Wales and Cardiff and his first cap against Australia. He told me about his days at Llanelli and more.

'I told him I used to travel up from the Valleys to watch him play for Wales and I told him about when I'd first met him getting off the players' bus in Llanelli when Cardiff played there in 1969. I was playing for the county Under-15s that day and we played in the morning and I had the autographs of himself, Gareth Edwards and Delme Thomas.

'I looked up at the clock and it was now 5am. Barry talked more about rugby, he was enjoying himself and we were on first-name terms now, Gyp and The King, mun!

'I was knackered and tired but no way was I going to bed with this once-in-a-lifetime personal interview with The King. So it was more beer and more rugby.

'Anyway, at 6.30am I finally said, "Barry, I have to go to bed, I'm knackered!"

'"No bach, it's not worth it now, breakfast will be at 7am, join me please?"

'"OK," I said, and we sat down for breakfast, with Barry still talking rugby. He finally went to leave and I got up and put out my hand to shake. He said, "No give us a cwtch, mun!"

'He signed some autographs for my mother on a hotel bill and I left my address for him. He said he would send me an autographed photo.

'I thought, "The boys will never believe this, never, never – a night with The King."

'I crawled to bed fucked and pissed. I was only asleep for an hour and the fucking maid was knocking to clean the room. I said I'd only just got to bed and gave her £20 and said, "Please don't wake me till the afternoon."

'Some months after, an envelope turned up. Inside was a Triple Crown 1969 blazer badge and a Cardiff RFC blazer badge. There was no message but I knew who it was from.

'I met Barry a few times after that in the ex-players' lounge at the stadium. He was a great person and I have photos with him because that was the day The Gyp met The King!

'Don't know if you can use it butty, but what a story! Gyp xxx.'

Well, I have used it and it reflects so much of that 1970s era of Welsh rugby greatness and the down-to-earth humility of both Barry John and Gyp.

I don't think it's any accident that Barry John's father worked down the pit at Cefneithin. Barry John has now sadly passed away but I have a sneaky feeling he would have endorsed Gyp's legendary status too.

A lot has been written about the deification of Welsh rugby heroes and some rail against the maleness and macho culture that has ruled the sport. But here we just have two men happily enjoying a beer and a long sozzled chat about sport. That's OK, isn't it?

It was still sport then too, without the money that has corrupted any activity in this modern age where every celebrity chauffeurs forth from his gated mansion (and it is still largely a 'he' who reaps all the rewards to be had). Children dream of being a celebrity first and foremost, rather than a skilled team player. They want the YouTuber fast track to fame and fortune.

Meanwhile, back at the bar, Gyp and Barry John were just having a pint and a cwtch and telling it how it was the day Gyp met The King.

He's always there if you need him on the phone. He'll always talk to you. He's helped me no end when I've been really very down. I was really struggling. He's always there for people. He's an exceptional man.

David @Caerau Men's Shed

Mental health
and well-being

WHEN STRONG MEN like Gyp are prepared to talk about their mental health and depression, it is a loud and clear message to the rest of us. During the sessions to put this book together, Gyp has never been afraid to let emotion take hold of him. He's done that with demonstrable anger when he's stuck up for workers as their union rep, but he's also done it through tears when he recalls the pain of childhood and his mother and father's struggles with their own mental health. He creased up in conversation with me once, recalling some of the pain other men in the Shed have shared with him.

Every time he meets me, he puts his huge arms around me and hugs me to him and kisses me on the top of the head.

In many ways, Gyp sees the Caerau Men's Shed as recreating a little bit of that camaraderie of the mines. He knows that since the pits have closed the Valleys have had the stuffing knocked out of them. It was an act of political vandalism and there was no plan or vision for how the communities would reinvent themselves. That reinvention is an on-going part of the miner's struggle for people like Gyp.

The Men's Shed movement and other voluntary

Gyp with some of the boys from Caerau Men's Shed.

groups like them, have sprung up in many communities to try and offer some hope and some meaning, to try and engender some form of community spirit. During the pandemic Gyp and his other Men's Shed colleagues were busy throughout, delivering food parcels and shopping for those in need.

Gyp is well aware that there are lots of people struggling and suffering with all manner of mental health issues. He wants to reach out and offer a sense of belonging and a sense of purpose.

The Shed is now open every day. It used to be open on Fridays, but Gyp and the committee realised people are lonely every day and there needs to be things out there and places where they can go. Gyp is the first one to sing the praises of other committee members and the importance of everyone playing a vital part in delivering services to the community.

The Friday meeting still involves a hot meal at the

The 2023 front cover of the Caerau Men's Shed calendar.

Dyffryn Chapel, and it remains a popular day for all.

Gyp is a little reluctant to talk about his own struggles, but I nudge him a little and he tells me this by email: 'I had been suffering from severe depression. I will not go into details because everyone who suffers has different symptoms, but people who have experienced this know what it's like.

'I needed to get active and be more social again to start improving my self-worth. I was aware of a group meeting at Noddfa in Caerau that called themselves the Men's Shed. So one day I decided that this might be what I needed to try and drag me out of the black hole I had found myself in.

'Sure enough, I found there a great compassion for fellow men that had been suffering from all kinds of health issues, with some suffering or having suffered from depression which helped a lot in my case. There were only eight members there when I started, some of these I already knew through rugby or working in the mines.

'I began to realise the extent of the effect of these illnesses they were suffering, and realised that there must be many more similar men out in the community. We only met once a week but I thought surely people were suffering from being isolated and lonely every day of the week.

'Anyway, in a while I felt very comfortable there and decided to do more. An AGM was called and I was proposed as the chairman. I then got to work with the help of the committee to move the Shed forward, and more members followed. We increased our numbers to sixteen members and we needed more for them to do.

'The idea of producing a calendar was born, along with crafts, woodwork and talks from guest speakers and all at a place they could come to every day when they felt like it.

'As we grew, we moved our meetings to CDT (Caerau Development Trust) and this gave us

Gyp receiving a Mayor's award in March 2019 for his contribution to his community.

129

more room plus the freedom for our members to meet on other days of the week.

'Our membership quickly grew to twenty-five and we were given a container that we turned into a small workshop. But pretty soon this became too small for our needs. Luckily, we had secured funding to look for proper workshop premises which in time became the Caerau Men's Shed Workshop Project.

'We continued to work for the community throughout the Covid pandemic, delivering food parcels for those in need and the whole community got to know who Caerau Men's Shed really were!

'Our work in the community has continued as we are always making gates, fences and other items for people who are in need, and everything is made at affordable prices out of recycled wood. A lot of work has been carried out to make us sustainable for the future so that others can follow the path we have started.

'I believe mental health issues are going to rise significantly following the pandemic and other mounting pressures. The Men's Shed will be there as a sanctuary for those that are struggling.

'We have produced four calendars, a Shed diary and printed two poetry books written by Keith Dixon, an eighty-five-year-old Shed member known affectionately as Dixie. We've also started our own drama group called 'Shed Full of Laughter' and we performed a successful play to a full house at the Senedd. We have a walking football group and a gym group and we continue to do a large amount of work for the community.

'Caerau Men's Shed was proud to have the oldest

member of any Men's Shed in the world in Mr Victor Davies, until he sadly passed away last year at the wonderful age of 103 years old.

'This year Caerau Men's Shed received a Mayor's Citizenship Award recognising us for our work in the community. There are some members who work tirelessly for the Shed and we must remember they are all volunteers. It is always a team effort.

'It makes me very proud.'

Gyp is certainly not alone as someone who has struggled in the Valleys of south Wales.

A report in the medical journal *The Lancet* in 2014 stated that: 'The former mining towns of the south Wales Valleys have one of the highest levels of antidepressant prescribing in Wales... as many as one in six of its residents are on antidepressants, the highest prescribing rate in the UK.'

The article goes on to quote Rob Poole, Professor of Social Psychiatry at Bangor University, who says: 'People in poverty are unhappy – that's a reality. But we have extended the limits of depression, and we now see it as a clinical phenomenon, rather than a life phenomenon... Over the years the social capital – mutual societies and social clubs built around the pits – have been picked away. Those networks have disappeared.'

The Lancet article also referred to another report from 2014, and said: 'A report comparing former mining communities across the UK found that the south Wales Valleys perform the worst on nearly every socio-economic measure... the incapacity benefit claimant rate in the former south Wales coalfields is 11.2 per cent compared

I wouldn't answer the door or the phone. I was on medication and felt suicidal. It's (Men's Sheds) changed my life completely.

Christopher Davies

Gyp's personal story, used to advertise the Men's Shed and get other men talking.

to the south-east England rate of 4.5 per cent. Around forty per cent of incapacity benefit claims are for mental health problems.'

Nobody wants to tar the region as completely without hope and be constantly banging on about how bad things are... that only makes matters worse. But as with any problem, you have to understand it fully before solutions can ultimately be found. The seeds of recovery are everywhere.

There has been a move towards social prescribing. This approach is about connecting someone to activities, groups and services in their area. It is an approach that offers community ventures that link people together and build friendships and partnerships. Numerous voluntary groups (like the Men's Shed and Lads and Dads) have grown up to extend a hand to those who are struggling.

Gyp gets it. He understands his community and all

the daily struggles. He never forgets the hardships of the strikes. He never forgets his own demons that nearly drove him to complete despair. He knows he was so close to the edge without barely any hope.

As we talk more, weeks after his previous comments about his own mental health, Gyp opens up again and emails me more about his depression, some things he had told me previously but now with another context:

'I was at my lowest ebb when my marriage broke up. At around that time my mother died and then my father died. And I lost my job through redundancy.

'I was staring depression full in the face.

'I had panic attacks and I piled the weight on. At one point I got up to twenty-six stone.

'I went on anger management classes and I went to bereavement classes.

'I had real drinking problems.

'I was in a dark, dark place, butty.

'I wouldn't answer the phone.

'I wouldn't answer the door.

'I was awake all night and I'd sleep all day.

'I wouldn't walk far, I'd lost my confidence.

'I'd lost my self-worth.

'Sometimes I had thoughts of suicide.

'I have come a long way since those dark days, butty.

'Gyp xx.'

As we get closer to printing and publishing I get yet another email from Gyp and they're always welcome. I don't think the stories will ever stop coming. This time Gyp offers me a piece of his own writing from the time in his life when he was really down. It is something he has kept. He says he wrote it at his lowest ebb when he was firmly in the grip of depression:

Let not the dark one consume you

I have crawled on my belly in the darkness below, down in the bowels of the earth, and I've been consumed by its black choking dust that burns your eyes like hot pokers and turns your lungs to stone or sponge.

I have sweated blood and tears, with muscles aching and screaming to hew the black diamonds that are used to stoke the devil's furnace, not knowing the price you have to pay to the keeper of souls. For it becomes like a drug and makes you crave more.

There is no escape from this pit of The Dark One. He cares not if you are old or young, he taketh the righteous and the sinner. They are both cast into the fiery furnace.

I have also become consumed by alcohol and cast to the depths of despair and darkness. The darkness becomes my friend. I know in my mind this is not right but I see no light to lead me out from under this dark shadow that shrouds me. I know not who I am any more?

Years pass, it becomes a part of my life now. There is no day or night, it all merges into one. I am not alone in this darkness. I am joined by others that have also been consumed with eyes that once burned bright but are now reduced to only a dim flicker. I am losing family and friends. I cannot take any more of this nightmare.

Hope comes like the wind.

I reach for hope and grasp it with both hands. I hold on tight and never let go and I ride on the wings of hope until the old warriors who are survivors of this darkness come to rescue me. They are strong, caring, compassionate and understanding. I have the feeling I will be saved.

I ride on the wings of hope to the light that I had been seeking. I am saved, exhausted, but saved I will better myself.

I too have now become a warrior able to save the ones that stumble into the darkness. But I still carry the scars as a reminder of that Hell. It is me.

This is who I am!

It is Gyp's own struggles and his honesty that are the essence of his story for me. He has learnt from his own battles and has always been desperate to help others. His life now is dedicated to his locality, to his community.

It is worth taking a moment to recall what Credi the gypsy told young Christopher Davies as a six-year-old boy: 'You will become a great leader and be loved by many, but this will weigh heavily on your heart because your heart will be so laden with love.'

He's got a heart of gold but sometimes he can certainly be a bit stubborn. He really likes to help people, which is fantastic.

What you see with Gyp is what you get.

I met him through the Men's Shed and if there's anything wrong he's there for you through difficult times.

I count him as a genuine friend.

Brian @Caerau Men's Shed

Getting to know you

When we were writing this book I wanted to make sure I covered all the bases and got into the deepest, darkest corners of Gyp's life and character. He is brutally honest with me and I knew he wouldn't shy away from anything I asked him, so I thought I'd try a homemade questionnaire to see if it picked up any areas I might have missed. I wanted to be sure I gave you the inner Gyp and we really got to the heart of what makes him tick.

The results of my questions did throw up some surprising and thought-provoking answers, along with the inevitable stories that made me laugh (sex and the Salvation Army!) and, regarding his tough and resilient Mam, there were bits that brought a tear to my eye too.

So here's the questionnaire with Gyp's answers:

What is your idea of perfect happiness?
My idea of perfect happiness is world peace and more love to humankind and animals… and of course Wales beating England at rugby!

What is your most embarrassing moment?
My most embarrassing moment was being caught having sex by my mother, who entered the room with five ladies from the Salvation Army.

If you were an animal, what animal would you be?
I would like to be a dolphin, free to roam the seven seas full of energy and life.

What are your views on God?
My views on God are that there is a higher being created by people's inner emotions and senses, and it's what you call on at those lowest times in your life.

What are your best qualities?
My best quality is me trying to care and love my fellow human beings and animals.

What do you most dislike about yourself?
I do not dislike anything about myself. I am who I am and I am happy with that.

What part has love played in your life?
Love is what the whole wide world sometimes seems too short of... it is powerful and it's the energy that motivates life itself... without love we really have nothing at all.

What childhood experience comes to mind?
The first experience that comes to mind is of losing the ones you love and not understanding why. That was the worst pain I ever suffered in my life.

What is the biggest challenge that faces you in life?
Life itself is always a challenge from the cradle to the grave. We all face our own battles in different ways. One of my more recent challenges has been accepting getting

older and accepting the things you can't do any more as you get older. But I am still here battling on... many of my dead butties would change places with me in an instant if it was possible.

What do you fear the most?
I fear the dark place that I was once engulfed by in that pit of lost souls.

If you could live your life again, what would you do differently?
If I had done things differently I may not have become the man I am today. I am very happy with the person who I have become and I always strive to be a better me.

What's your view on ghosts?
I have more trouble with the living than I do with ghosts. I think I am OK with the ghosts and I think the ghosts are OK with me.

The next ones are where Gyp just finishes off the sentences:

My mother and I...
My mother was my rock and the glue that held our family together, I loved her dearly. Did I tell you the story of when I lost my first-ever pay packet at the pit?

Some old colliers took me to the pub (the Dyffryn Hotel) to play three-card brag and I lost all my very first week's wages. I had to go home and tell my mam, who was all excited and waiting for my first week's lodge.

'Mam,' I said. 'I have no pay.'

'Why is that boy?' she asked.

'I had to pay for the timber I used.'

'It's oOK boy,' she said. 'Don't worry.'

The next day when I came home there was £7.50 on the dinner table.

'What's that, Mam?' I asked.

'It's your wages you lost playing cards. I went up the Dyffryn pub and had your money back off those colliers who took it and I gave them a piece of my mind. Remember boy, I am a collier's wife so I know what goes on in the pubs on a Friday at the end of a shift. Timber my arse!'

People think I am...

People think that I am a legend and they say that, but I am just Gyp Davies, nothing more and nothing less.

My father...

My father is still my hero, I loved him endlessly.

I want my grandchildren to...

I want my grandchildren to love and care for people like I have.

Secretly I...

Secretly I am a Welsh Warrior.

One thing I can't stand is...

One thing I can't stand is bullies.

When somebody makes fun of me...

When someone makes fun of me I laugh along with them.

My dream is...

My dream is always for world peace and for everyone in Wales to be able to speak in their native tongue.

Sometimes I feel like...

Sometimes I feel sad, sometimes I feel elated. Sometimes I am tired, sometimes I am happy. Like everyone else I feel different emotions but that's life I suppose. I feel thankful I am able to do the things I am doing and, more than anything, I love helping people.

I don't like the sort of people who...

I like all people. It's just that some are different than others. I suppose there are people who do not like me but I just think, 'Join the end of the queue, butty.'

I'm not here to be liked, I am here to HELP!

Our family...

My family is my life, the bond, the reason I am who I am.

Being popular is...

I am not popular... I am Gyp, being popular is not what I am here for.

No one can make me...

No one can make me eat olives, LOL.

You can build a community by...

You can build a community by caring for each other and respecting each other. You do it by understanding the needs of others. We need to love the beauty of the valleys and the people who live there.

I am sorry when...

I am sorry when a friend or loved one dies.

The one thing I've tried to do in my life is...

The one thing I have tried to do in my life is to make myself a better person than what I was.

I've tried to help people who are struggling to make ends meet. I've tried to comfort the hurt and to be there when life is too much.

I have come to understand what my purpose in life is and I think it is to help the ones who struggle, including me, and I am happy to do that.

Gyp Davies xx

The guy goes non-stop. What an engine on him! When everyone else wants to sit down, he's like, 'Right lads let's get on with it.'

Without him the Men's Shed wouldn't be where it is today, he's the driving force.

Nigel Rigden @Caerau Men's Shed

Caerau Men's Shed

THE MEN'S SHED movement is worth a little more exploration and especially the Gyp-led version.

Firstly, in case you're not familiar with Caerau, it might be worth knowing a little bit about the area where Gyp's whole life takes place. Caerau is a mining village (ex-mining village now) just up the valley from Maesteg in the Bridgend Borough.

If you look at the *Welsh Index of Multiple Deprivation* of 2019, Caerau ranks in the top five areas of deprivation within the whole of Wales. It is ranked at number one as the most deprived area in terms of health (keep going to Billy's Gym, Gyp!). Even more worryingly Caerau has become more and more deprived with every publication of the index since 2005.

Caerau is a tough place to live according to the stats.

The Men's Shed movement began in Australia in 1998 (some date it as earlier than that). It is a simple and effective idea based on the notion of a garden shed where a man might go to carry out tasks such as mending a lawn mower or restoring a piece of furniture.

The concept has grown into a worldwide movement with the slogan 'Shoulder to Shoulder' because 'men don't talk face to face, they talk shoulder to shoulder'. In some senses the Sheds could be seen as a reincarnation

Men's Shed calendar photo, with a nod to many of their mining backgrounds.

of the workingmen's clubs of the nineteenth century that were so popular in industrial Britain.

I hope you can see the attraction for a man like Gyp who was struggling and missing that workplace camaraderie he'd always been a part of.

A fundamental difference for the present-day 'Shedders' has been in the growth of the 'health by stealth' approach associated with the Men's Shed movement. At long last men have permission to talk openly about their mental health, which has for so long been such a difficult area to address. We only have to think back to the struggles that Gyp's father had coming back from traumatic wartime experiences to realise that men have been left to flounder and 'man up'. That culture is now what can only be described as 'toxic masculinity' which goes hand in hand with the drinking culture that Gyp

Caerau Men's Shed performing their drama *The Full Ponty* at the Senedd.

has talked about. Despite these recent improvements, there is still a long, long way to go.

Caerau Men's Shed has continued to evolve and develop. They have recently opened a new workshop facility where local people can bring things to be mended by the boys at the Shed.

The genius of Gyp, though, is that he has an open mind to the direction the Shed can take, so that men can be both teachers and learners. They now have opportunities to act on stage as well as to make and repair.

My first real involvement with the Men's Shed movement was working to cultivate memories and stories of their time down the pit (and it turned out to include many other trades too). That then led to another project where they wanted me to get them acting and direct them, so they could do a mini tour with a piece of drama that was written by one of their friends. We improvised around that text and gave the drama a title of *The Full Ponty*, which should tell you everything!

Not one of them had ever acted before and getting them to walk on stage in a sexy manner to Tom Jones singing 'You Can Leave Your Hat On' was an experience I will treasure. They performed the piece in three places to big audiences, including the Senedd where they received a wonderful ovation.

The local Assembly Member said it was the only time he'd ever seen a virtually naked man in the Welsh parliament, he was only wearing a fluorescent green mankini and strutting his stuff to Hot Chocolate's 'You Sexy Thing'. That is another image that will stay with me too!

Their drama club is now flourishing and they've found a director for the club and have a new piece in rehearsal.

As noted both Gyp and myself have agreed that if there are any profits made from this book, they will all go to support the wonderful and varied work of the Caerau Men's Shed, supporting men's mental health and well-being.

He's an absolute header. He nagged me for two years to join the Shed. He's a born leader. I got to be honest if it wasn't for him this place wouldn't still be going.
Bill @Caerau Men's Shed

I've known him four years now and he's so dedicated.

Dixie @Caerau Men's Shed

He's a good leader. I've not known him long but he's a good man, loyal to everyone. He does great work for Men's Shed and for the community. It's a pity there weren't more like him.

Billy @Caerau Men's Shed

Life Beyond the Shed Door

THE CAERAU MEN'S Shed has produced three calendars that would make some blush, but they certainly entertain and bring a smile to so many in the community. Many have been bought to support the tremendous work of the Shed.

In 2019 the calendar was accompanied by a little book called *Life Beyond the Shed Door*. This book was an amalgamation of many stories told by the boys and tries to paint a picture that captures something of the atmosphere of the Shed.

We used a narrator's voice for the diary to represent someone who might be a reluctant first-time attender, just as Gyp himself was when he discovered the Shed and found out how supportive it could be to him at a time when he was struggling.

Places like the Caerau Men's Shed have gained in value and now, along with many other community groups, they have linked up with politicians and are pushing for greater services to be mapped out and used in a social prescribing model as a way forward for dealing with well-being and mental health.

According to a report by NHS Public Health Wales, *Social Prescribing in Wales*, in May 2018: 'There is increasing acceptance that sources of support in local communities have an important role to play alongside clinical care or even as an alternative in improving someone's individual health and well-being outcomes. Well-being services offer people a wide range of sources of support within the community, improving emotional and physical well-being and reducing social isolation.'

The large-scale cuts to so many local services in recent years have led to a resurgence of so many inspired volunteers and voluntary projects. These groups are so often born out of a real and very genuine desire to make communities better.

The pitfalls identified are around funding for those groups, often being short-term, and there may be some duplication and some very well-meaning groups may end up fighting over the same pots of money. They may also find private companies offering similar services will spring up to gain contracts for local funding. The general growth of tendering in the care sector has often been corrosive, as it can lead to a race to the bottom as private operations undercut each other to gain contracts.

With regard to the calendar and the booklet *Life Beyond the Shed Door*, we have included many of the photographs from the photo-shoots in this book and we've also included the Shed Diary as an appendix item to Gyp's story, as we thought you might want to read some of the other men's stories too, alongside this one.

A favourite tale from the Shed Diary, for all of us, was the story of the young lad caught 'necking' by the police in the 1950s. It has been recounted in various speeches by many people now, and it seems unbelievable that it was originally told by an earnest octogenarian called Ted!

Here's a section of that bit from the diary, just to whet your appetite:

Dear Diary,

Have you ever wondered how much of a journey it can be to find true love?

I heard a youngster talking about dating this week, talking about this site and that and scrolling through pictures for the ones you like. I was telling the men at the Shed about it and we got talking.

Well it wasn't like that in our day, we didn't have the luxury of photos, and someone mentioned Merthyr where they'll tell you all about their 'monkey parading'.

We used to call it 'courting' rather than dating. You call it that now and people think you've been arrested for something, courting has become stalking as one of the boys said!

Mind you, one of the lads remembers taking a girl home one night and getting friendly in the back lanes and a copper caught them:

'What you doing?' he said.

'We're necking,' said the lad.

'Well,' he said, 'put your neck back in your trousers and bugger off home!'

Ted's wonderful story of romance goes way back to the days before dating sites, the internet, Tinder and all that malarkey. The whole of the booklet *Life Beyond the Shed Door* is included at the back of this book.

SOUTH WALES MINERS' MUSEUM

PRESENTS

ALONG WITH LLYNFI EX MINERS & CAERAU MEN'S SHED

A COAL MINERS

REUNION

FRIDAY, 19TH NOVEMBER 2021

DOORS OPEN 6.30PM

JOIN US AT MAESTEG RFC FOR A COAL MINERS REUNION
A GREAT EVENING TO CATCH UP WITH PAST WORK
COLLEAGUES TO REMINISCE AND ENJOY A PINT!
FEATURING THE WONDERFUL
MAESTEG GLEEMEN MALE VOICE CHOIR

VENUE
Maesteg RFC
Llynfi Road
CF34 9DS

For More Information or Gain Tickets Contact
The Museum on 01639 851833 or Email
info@south-wales-miners-museum.co.uk

He's a good bloke is Gyp, he'll help anybody out who's in trouble. I find him alright. The Men's Shed would have died years ago without him.

Andrew Cocks (Grit) @Caerau Men's Shed

He does everything for everyone, and now he's a councillor he's learning how to overcome bureaucracy, and if it can be done Gyp will go out of his way to get it done. He has so many contacts, he knows everyone. And as Chairman of the Men's Shed he's so active and uses his ways to inspire people... and, I should add, if there are any empty pallets knocking around he'll find them and get the wood for the recycling projects in the Shed!

Nigel Williams @Caerau Men's Shed

Politician

THE MOST RECENT chapter for Gyp is that in the last year he took the plunge and decided to stand for election as a local councillor.

He felt incensed by seeing other councillors cutting the ribbons and opening food banks. All the passion of defending pits and livelihoods had now been reduced to an official acceptance of hand-outs and charity for the poor and vulnerable. This seemed a moral outrage and against everything that Gyp had fought for all his life. He does not believe we should tolerate the very existence of food banks.

It made Gyp see red and he's now grappling with a completely new world of council decisions and council business. He's already tearing his hair out trying to find out how best to get things done.

But now they've gone and made him the Mayor of Maesteg for 2024. What a journey for the boy who did errands to get sixpence so he could have his future told to him! What a future it has turned out to be!

He's not content with just making waves in the political arena but also remains active in other areas too. He sings in a choir and was the chairman for a stint there. He's in the Men's Shed almost every day and he's driving forward new initiatives. He's the chair of the Llynfi Ex-Miners' Support Group and has been a school governor in two schools.

Gyp as Mayor.

One thing is very plain for anyone who knows Gyp – while he has breath in his body he will fight for the people of his community and stand alongside them through thick and thin.

I'm not sure we make people like Gyp any more. He is, as he always says, a dying breed, but on meeting him you can't help thinking the world needs more like Gyp... or maybe it's his values and sense of belonging that we all need to pay heed to.

I've heard of his vicious temper but all I've seen is a heart of gold. He's there willing to help anybody out. In my opinion you can't fault him and he's such a good leader.

Ted @Caerau Men's Shed

Epilogue

THE VETERANS FROM the First World War (like my grandfather and Gyp's grandfather) are all gone and the veterans from the Second World War (like my father and Gyp's father) are virtually all gone now too.

Gyp is well aware that the miners will be next, that they are a dying breed, a battle-weary group of older men, many of whom were sacrificed at places like Senghenydd in 1914 (439 men died) and Six Bells in 1960 (forty-five men died) – one disaster that happened 100 years ago and the other sixty-four years ago. There is a long list of disasters and death, many of which will be familiar to you.

In total over 6,000 miners have died in recorded accidents in pits in Wales, but this is only estimated to be seventeen per cent of the total numbers of miners who have died from working underground. When you also add to that the huge numbers that died from mining-related illnesses, then the total would be much, much higher.

If you put it alongside the figure of 15,000 Welsh men who are estimated to have died in the Second World War, you get a sense of the scale of sacrifice men made on a daily basis at their workplace deep underground. Until 1842 you can also include women and children in those losses as well.

As Gyp says (and he borrowed some of the words from a man called Jenkins): 'When they demanded every ton and lump of coal that could be so brutally hewn from deep under the ground, it was never intended, according to the laws of nature, for man, boy or beast to spend so much of their lives underground.

'But it was coal that put the food on the table, put the clothes on our back and the shoes on the feet of our children. It was coal that gave our people pride, made our communities strong and worthy of respect.

'None of it would have been possible without the women of the Valleys, the mothers and daughters, the homemakers back then.

'It's one hell of a story that must be told to future generations whose feet gently tread above the underground world of coal.'

Now we live in a world where the climate crisis is very real and it's the biggest challenge facing people living on earth right now. It will only be overcome by people working together and reducing their own tendencies towards greed and ensuring they have their own needs met at all costs.

The camaraderie and togetherness of those miners is much needed now, their sense of looking out for each other, their sense of community and their faith in education. Most miners wanted to keep their sons out of the pit, they wanted a better future.

Coal's time is over and politicians (like Gyp!) now have to find ways to engender those very special community values that were so evident in the towns and villages of the south Wales Valleys during the coal boom. They were evident again, to an extent, during the Covid pandemic and we have to find ways to continually build and nurture communities where everyone thrives.

This story of Gyp's life shows us the patterns that exist in all our lives as we follow in the footsteps of all those who went before. The mines had existed for so long and Gyp was so keen to follow all his ancestors down the pit.

But this story also highlights that painful ending to those pit communities and the suffering many have endured.

Caerau scores so high on every deprivation index but there is more to a community than facts and figures. There is a resilience and a stubbornness that is evident in much of the local area. Gyp personifies that stubbornness and strength. There are groups and initiatives doing their utmost to nurture the green shoots of a recovery, offering opportunities to children and adults, keeping that spirit of the miners and their resolute wives well and truly alive.

Community certainly still exists and, as Gyp said earlier in this book: 'It's not going to be easy but who said it would be?'

Christopher Davies is certainly fighting on for Nantyffyllon, for Caerau and for Bridgend. He gives everything he's got to the Men's Shed and now to the political arena. As noted, in 2024 he became the Mayor of Maesteg. Whoever would have thought a boy who ate vinegar and toothpaste sandwiches would make it to the very top of the pile in Bridgend County Borough?!

As he says himself, he will keep giving to his community

until his very last breath and then he'll be buried, as 'Gyp' Davies, maybe the last of a dying breed.

Gyp's story belongs to all of us and he wants nothing more than for all of us to have ownership of it. It is his story and it is our story and it's one that should be told over and over.

I don't really know what to say about my race. I'm so proud of them and I love the Welsh with a passion that's almost idolatrous, particularly the south Welsh who are the people I know best and particularly the mining class of the south Welsh.

I believe that they speak rather better than most people I've ever met in all my life. I believe that they're blazingly honest, I believe that they're careful, watchful, that they don't give away emotion too quickly or too easily.

If the chips were down and the world was to come to an end and I was in dead trouble and people said, 'Who would you like to have with you? What sort of people?' I'm afraid I would have to say, chauvinistically, the Welsh miner.

Richard Burton, Welsh actor, 1925–1984

Everyone you meet always asks if you have a career, are married, or own a house as if life was some kind of grocery list. But no one ever asks you if you are happy.

Heath Ledger, Australian actor, 1979–2008

I've known Christopher Louis Charles Davies for over fifty years. Who? I hear some of you ask.

'Gyp', mun; but I didn't think I was able to say that. We were John Street and Brown Street boys from Nantyfyllon,

we went to school together, we played some sport together and we spent our summers camping up Garnwen Mountain together.

Our career paths moved in different directions as he went from Coegnant Colliery to the Bridgend paper mill and I went from being a local PE teacher to a Rugby Development Officer for the Scarlets. It was at this stage that we rekindled our links and we were a great partnership visiting schools and coaching rugby skills to children. We worked as effectively as a double act, entertaining and coaching children at the same time.

It is a measure of the partnership that, when I went back to a school without him, the children would immediately ask, 'Where's Gyp?' and I'd say that he was working, to which they'd reply, 'That's so disappointing, we like Gyp.'

'Everyone likes Gyp,' I hear you say and I'd agree.

However, if you were an adversary on the rugby field, there are many men that wouldn't agree with us. Nevertheless, that's a different story and there's a book to be written on his escapades on a rugby field; that's one for adults only.

There are many ways you can judge the quality of a person. For me a key judgement is to see how prepared someone is to give up their time so that others can benefit. In his roles with the Men's Shed and as a local councillor, Christopher Louis Charles Davies provides so much proof of that. I'm so proud to call him my friend.

Dai Arthur, lifelong friend

Appendix:
Life Beyond the Shed Door

Cover of booklet which was a
partnership between Caerau Men's
Shed and Awen Cultural Trust.

Dear Diary,

You get to a certain age... I'm never quite sure when that is because nobody knows their actual departure date do they? But it's a certain age when there seems to be more to look back on than there is to look forward to and, for some people, all their hopes have turned to regrets.

Anyway I think I might have got there!

So it was interesting a few weeks ago when someone

told me about the Men's Shed and said I might like to go along.

'No not me,' I said, confident that I didn't need the company of other old hairy-backed blokes. I was quite happy whiling away the hours at home enjoying the fruits of my retirement. I didn't want to go down and whittle away at sticks with a load of grumpy old men.

But as the weeks passed it got mentioned again and I thought, Why not give it a go? You're never too old for a new experience and it's on my doorstep, plus I'm still a part of my community, aren't I?

So today was the day I ventured down, not really sure what to expect... and what a great welcome! All the boys gave me a handshake or a pat on the back and made me very relaxed. The banter flew around faster than a Valleys train from Cardiff (just above walking pace!).

They asked what I was interested in, and they said they can help me with my interest in photography. There is someone who works professionally and will help me to develop (pardon the pun). There is a portrait artist too who offered to help me with my drawing, so I'm hooked in and I'll show you the results as I go along.

I had a tidy meal and there was a meeting to discuss the calendar shoot and other projects. The calendar shoot is being done by the photographer. It involves carefully placed spades, carrots held in a strategic position so that your sausage and biscuits aren't exposed to the whole world during the thirty-one days of August. I can't wait!

I laughed more than I have for a long time and I'm going back next week to see if there really is such a thing as a mankini.

Dear Diary,

Have you ever wondered how much of a journey it can be to find true love?

I heard a youngster talking about dating this week, talking about this site and that and scrolling through pictures for the ones you like. I was telling the men at the Shed about it and we got talking.

Well it wasn't like that in our day, we didn't have the luxury of photos, and someone mentioned Merthyr where they'll tell you all about their 'monkey parading'.

We used to call it 'courting' rather than dating. You call it that now and people think you've been arrested for something, courting has become stalking as one of the boys said!

Mind you, one of the lads remembers taking a girl home one night and getting friendly in the back lanes and a copper caught them:

'What you doing?' he said.

'We're necking,' said the lad.

'Well,' he said, 'put your neck back in your trousers and bugger off home!'

It wasn't always easy meeting girls back in our day, you see. You might go to a dance hall but you'd need to be able to dance properly. Jiving was a good way to meet girls and I remember I had a lovely pair of winkle-pickers. You could get arrested just for saying that these days too.

But you went out hunting in packs; you have to remember there were no women down the pit. We relied on youth clubs, school discos, dances and chapel.

And everything you did got round the village in half an hour.

The cinema was popular on a first date. We had three in Maesteg back then, the Plaza, the Regal and the New Theatre, and we had the Cosy in Caerau and it was cosy, too. The back seats were the hottest ones in town, it was all happening back there.

I remember once I had to hide from Sandra. She wouldn't leave me alone, and then once I got hit by a brush just for chatting with a girl!

We all used to smoke at fourteen or fifteen back then, smoking was seen as the cool thing to do and there was underage drinking and everyone knew you were underage. Tommy Farr's brother even hid us from the police in his cellar!

No self-respecting bloke drank halves back then, it had to be a pint. We can remember the vicar who got too fond of the drink, hard to say if he was a proper alcoholic but everyone liked him. We remember when a double BACARDI and Coke cost just sixpence.

We didn't have to worry about all those drugs and trouble they have on a night out these days. You might have the odd punch-up for being in the wrong place at the wrong time, but it was nothing sinister, no knives and baseball bats.

Everything would be as innocent as 'My friend Suzy wants to know if you'll come and sit by her?'

We chased the chambermaids and the waitresses and it all seemed harmless enough, perhaps a bit of groping and fumbling in the back lane.

Even the music was quite simple and innocent back

then too. The Beatles sang about wanting to hold your hand, Elvis couldn't help falling in love, and the Supremes asked you to stop in the name of love before you break my heart.

I'm not sure if it's better or worse these days, but I'll stick with courting rather than those dating websites.

Anyway, I'm not sure my winkle-pickers still fit me!

Dear Diary,

Went down the Men's Shed today. I say Shed but it's actually a room in a community centre. Anyway, we got talking about the old days (just for a change) and started reminiscing about how we never had a couch potato childhood. All our activities were always outside and we were always on the go.

We started thinking about how fit we used to be as kids. We'd think nothing of walking to Maesteg or running to Pontycymmer. We spent our childhoods on Shank's pony. In the summertime we'd go out at eight in the morning to play and come back at six at night.

You learnt a lot in the woods.

We'd take two big doorstop sandwiches, an inch thick with a bit of meat or fish paste, and a bottle of council pop. When we got older we'd have black sarnies down the pit, our hands were dirty but the coal was sterile. Some men would chew on coal for indigestion.

Nothing got wasted when we were young. We ate our crusts; in fact we ate anything to keep our stomachs full. There was no obesity crisis for the kids in those days, we were all skin and bone. We didn't know where our next meal was coming from half the time. There wasn't so much choice for food and often the fall-back position was good old egg and chips. The leftover bits made the bread and butter pudding and the chicken bones went into a soup – and don't even get Gordon started on his toenail wine and how he used a girl's knickers for a catapult! I don't know whether to believe a word he says but I could listen to him all day. He talks about the hook and wheel and claims Pontycymmer invented the penny-farthing. He should have his own TV show that man.

We made bikes from the ash cart and pieced together go-karts from the ash tip. We'd go down the mountain on a strip of lino or grease some cardboard with candle wax, and then you'd fly down that hill. We played on girders; we played down the pit and on building sites. There wasn't the same health and safety back then but if you hurt yourself you had to take it on the chin.

We made bows and arrows and peashooters and whistles. We all got chucked out of the pictures once for causing mayhem with our peashooters.

We'd use an old bed frame for the chassis of our go-karts. You might break your neck but you'd never break the kart. We had our knives and we'd carve our names but there was no danger in kids having knives back then. We used them properly and carved flutes and whittled sticks away.

One of the boys said he loved his old money box that he thought his dad had made for him. He only found out years later it was the meter box for the gas. If you didn't have a shilling for the meter you'd file a halfpenny down and it would do the trick.

Everyone had chores to do. We'd chop sticks and light the fires and fetch the coal. You'd take the pop bottles back to the pop man and claim the money but he was tight. He'd check to see if you'd got the bottles from the wrong street. One of the boys remembers his uncle delivering pop in a horse and cart. On a hot day, he'd sample the drink then top it up with water.

If you were lucky you might get the money to go and watch *Tarzan* at the cinema. We were a bit like Tarzan ourselves, we were the feral society but there was always love and a cwtch from your mam and you could bury yourself and be safe in her pinny.

Those were the days!

Dear Diary,

I got talking to one of the boys down at the Shed today. He started telling me about his life down the pits, stealing two ton of coal in a wheelbarrow when times were hard. He remembered those times as a sparky (electrician) when he skived off to the pit top to go trout fishing. He remembers pushing a 55-gallon drum of mineral oil up a 1 in 30 incline and asking if he could finish an hour earlier if he got it up there.

When he started down the pit everyone was asking about his family and who he belonged to. He was alright as his dad was a bit of a scrapper, but they hated his granddad because he was a means tester in the 1920s and 1930s and they told him to his face that his granddad was a 'bastard', even though he was just a young lad starting out. People were straight with each other back then, it was an honest community and you knew where you stood.

He was twenty-one years working down the pit and if he had the chance he said he'd go back down tomorrow; he loved the camaraderie and the banter. He remembers the '84 strike and those were tough times. He was in the Co-op car park asking people to donate what they could and collecting a few tins and money. An old lady came along and put 10p in his hand and took a tin of beans out!

There was another time when he was working in the miners' kitchen and a woman came in and asked, 'Have you got half a pound of lard to make chips?' and he was rushed off his feet, so jokingly told her, 'Aye, why don't you take the chip pan with you an all?' So she did! You couldn't make this stuff up.

When it all came to an end, he went for a job at Sony's in Bridgend in 1987 and the first question they asked in the interview was: 'So what do you think of Arthur Scargill?'

How does an honest miner answer that? I asked him what his reply was and he told me he said: 'If it was a perfect world, would it be worth living?'

He got the job.

Dear Diary,

Where does anyone really come from? I've been talking to a few of the boys at the Shed. There are boys from Cornwall, London way, and just about all over and even a vicar too! We are a mixed bunch for sure and all the better for it.

One thing we all have in common though is being settled in the Welsh Valleys now for the last leg of our journey (not the youngsters in the Shed, they may end up anywhere).

I love the fact that one bloke moved to Caerau from Cwm, near Ebbw Vale, and still we talked about his sense of belonging and where he's really from. Is he still a foreigner to Maesteg after 49 years?

The navvies came over from Ireland and still we talk about their hurling field in Caerau. Everyone in Maesteg has Irish relatives one way or another, plus of course we're all Europeans now!

The chap was telling me about his journey to Caerau. He remembers the time when Sean Connery was in the workingmen's club in Cwm. He doesn't mean so much these days, but he was a genuine star back then.

When the chap left school, the jobs were easy to come by. He remembers when you could go from one job to another in a day. There was Revlon, Silent Channel, Louis Edwards, Vitafoam, Porcelains of Italy and Christy Tyler's. A job at Gurnings back then was a job for life – but of course it's all changed, in fact it's a Morrisons job now. How times have moved on! The factories have all gone, disappearing into the Far Eastern horizon.

We talked together about how we wouldn't want to be a youngster growing up nowadays struggling to find hope. He told me he's always had an interest in model railways and probably has £10,000 worth of equipment up in his attic. It's not a huge leap from making aircraft parts for Concorde, is it? He loved his sport too, and was a keen cricketer. His finest moment of village cricket was taking seven wickets as a spin bowler, but his best mate still took the trouble to remind him he was crap at batting!

I then got talking to another fellow who said he definitely is 'Caerau-born and Caerau-bred, thick in the arm and thick in the head'.

He worked as a brickie for the council and told me a lovely story of how, one Christmas, they found an old piano and a chair, so they hoisted them up onto the van and drove round Bridgend singing carols to the general public and they loved it.

He then told me another story from 1992 when things were really tough and he was down to his last farthing. He told his wife to go and borrow money from his mum so they could survive and put money on their electric. But miracles happen to those who believe.

He was cleaning out a council flat with his mate and in the slats of the airing cupboard they found a tenner, then another, until they had £800 in a Co-op bag. There was money for the bills.

The next day they wondered if there might have been more, so they went back to check the skip where they'd dumped the furniture. He put his hand down the side of the sofa and pulled out a card. Inside it said: 'To Mal, all my love, Chris.'

It seemed a miracle of fate. He was Malcolm and Chris was his sister who'd died of cancer at forty-four and now it seemed she was helping her brother out from the other side. Miracles happen to those who believe.

Dear Diary,

Put your hand up if you remember your schooldays? That's what we were recalling at the Shed today.

But let's get the punishments out of the way first. You could be caned if you were found in no-man's-land between the girls' playground and the boys', especially if you were boasting about it underneath the headmaster's study!

One of the boys at the Shed said he was caned twenty-eight times in one thirty-five-minute lesson. That has to be a world record, doesn't it? And he said it only stopped when the bell went. Those were the days, eh? You could be caned for being late or just for the way you took the top off the milk bottle.

If the cane didn't get you the board rubber did, and it really hurt when they whipped you with that Bunsen burner tubing. There were teachers who had an unhealthy sadistic streak back in those days. One of the boys said he still sees one of his cruel teachers, who's now old and blind, up the doctor's surgery and has to work hard to stop himself from kicking that white stick away.

But some of the teachers had suffered too. Often they had war stories to tell and we'd get them going so we didn't have to work. One had elongated fingers from where he'd been stretched on the rack by the Japanese in the Second World War.

Back then in school, everything was alphabetical and you had to know your times tables. They'd fire questions at you on the spot. What is 8x7? What is 6x9?

We all remember our schooldays. A maths teacher would insist on seeing your workings-out in the margin.

A PE teacher would make you fight out your differences in the gym. A woodwork teacher would throw a block of wood at you and was proud that he never missed!

Schools were brutal back then. We were hit constantly with rulers and back-handers, there was no political correctness back then. A teacher would forever call to the ginger-haired boy, 'Now come here, Carrots.'

When we did escape, ten of us went trout fishing during the lunchtime. But the headmaster hooked us in when we got back to school and took two of the trout home for his tea. The Cornish member of our Shed told us he would nip off to go trainspotting and see the steam of the Cornish Riviera Express, a sight to be seen back then.

We had inkwells with blotting paper and blobs of ink. You'd flick pens and leave machine-gun blue stains across the back of another boy's clean white shirt.

Sometimes the best education came from family as we'd learn valuable lessons from our grans and our uncles. We finished school at 4pm and then left for good when we were fifteen years old. Then we had to learn quickly in the world of work. You might have been top dog in school, but you came bottom of the pile in work. The pits certainly sobered you up from all your childish silliness. Ted got a clip round the ear just for saying 'Oh bugger' down the pit. But the camaraderie of work was worth all the pain. It was hard industrial work and everyone helped anyone and watched each other's backs.

Back in those days women were mainly at home and the men worked, but things have changed. One thing that hasn't changed in our view is profit always seems to come before people. In fact, nowadays it does seem worse. It seems to be all 'me, me, me' and 'I, I, I' rather than 'us' and 'we'.

Nothing ever stays the same.

Children are more streetwise, they know what ketamine is and scroll their way through life. They can flick screens left and right but they struggle to find work. It seems like you need four A-levels just to get an interview for a cleaning job.

You just can't compare life back then with life today. We had satchels, caps, daps and blazers. Now they have computers, phones, drones and trainers.

Our times with teachers will always come and go but we all remember our schooldays.

Dear Diary,

Well, well, what a day at the Shed today! I met a poet and a gentleman still making us laugh at eighty-six years old. He had some stories to tell about his time down the pit and his time doing National Service.

He remembers the freedom of his childhood playing safely on the streets. He remembers his father in the Home Guard and the USA troops coming to stay. He has a clear memory of an American officer staying in their home and putting jam under his egg yolk and mixing it in.

All of his life this man has been writing poetry and recalled some of his poems and limericks that sum up his life. Firstly the one about the war that he wrote as a child in school:

Montgomery's the greatest of generals
The smallest and youngest of all
He's going to win all our battles
And drive Rommel out
Once and for all

Then there is the one that won him a limerick competition in which the WRU gave you the opening line:

There was a young man with no ticket
Who lay with his love in a thicket
When the moon shone on high
He said with a sigh
This is better than rugby or cricket!

And finally, his one for Boots the chemist in the 1980s that was on the topic of people's health and the dangers of smoking:

There was a young man who would smoke
Who thought giving up was a joke
But that was a blunder
He's now six foot under
With lungs like two lumps of coke

A real pleasure to listen to his stories and poems and long may he keep us entertained.

Dear Diary,

At the Shed today we got talking about Christmas (after all, it is the middle of summer!). God knows how we got onto it, but we remembered when we only got a few sweets or oranges and an apple in our pillowcase.

Nowadays children seem to dictate what they want.

We treasured our toys. We'd play with Dinky cars, then put them back in the box again when we finished.

The conversation moved back to how hard life was in those days.

Families were much bigger back then, eleven children in one family was not such a shock. Many might die of diseases like TB, in fact one of the lads lost all his family this way and had to go and live with an aunt. He survived and was in hospital where everyone was worried about catching it. They wore safety suits around him and everything.

He got cabin fever once though, on a hot day, and went off for a walk in his pyjamas. He walked round town from café to café where they gave him tea before returning to the hospital where he was promptly sent to bed! Until the age of fourteen he was given his own plate, knife, fork and cup and couldn't wash in the same place as others.

Hard times and hard lives.

And nothing could be harder than the pits, working on a seam that might be two-foot-six, where you had to lie on your side and the water would run through your shorts. One man told me how he was buried by a fall of coal. A big lump of it smashed him on the head and knocked him unconscious. He fell inches from a pool of water that would have drowned him. His friend Phil came and found him, a big man, six-foot-four, who carried him to the pithead and he was a month in hospital after fracturing five vertebrae in his neck.

There are many men in the Shed that have witnessed accidents underground. Now all the pits have gone and, sadly, many miners have gone with them.

Dear Diary,

That sense of community and camaraderie cropped up again today and this theme runs through Valleys life like the coal seams themselves.

We pride ourselves on our welcome in the Valleys and the Men's Shed is the same. It offers that sense of companionship where you can meet old and new friends and it puts a smile on your face.

We have a preacher in our number too, and some remember a time when the churches and chapels were full. Everyone went to chapel, you didn't want to embarrass your mother, and if you didn't go you'd miss the Sunday school trip to Porthcawl.

The gospel may be all about forgiveness but there are those that find it very hard to forgive Mrs Thatcher. The miners' strike of 1984 was a bitter moment and there are families that still struggle to get on because of it. The trade unions stood for the workers, there was a sense of pride as well as a sense of togetherness. We want politicians who lead from the heart, not from the wallet.

But still it sometimes seems like services are diminishing. We were glad to get rid of the soup kitchens but now they're coming back again with the food banks.

After the end of the Second World War every successive generation has seen themselves become better off but now that growth appears to have ended. It's all 'me, me, me' rather than 'we' and 'us' and 'our'.

Buses are gone, libraries are gone, road sweepers gone, sometimes you wonder if the Valleys have been left to slowly die?

The Men's Shed movement is a little oasis of hope. There has to be a fight-back and it has to start somewhere.

Dear Diary,

So where will it all end?

The internet runs the show now; we don't even need money any more. It's probably a good job as they're closing all the banks too!

But what about some of us oldies who struggle with the online experience? Sometimes I feel I have to change my password more often than my socks and that confuses the hell out of me. One of the boys said the internet is like a woman – it has the right to change its mind every week! [Nowadays I have to consider if he was being sexist with a comment like that too?]

A lot of us are at that age where we have to coax our legs to move and we're aching all over. We get off the bus and need to find the nearest toilet. If I could work the internet, I'd get an app to find the nearest toilet wherever I am. If we watch the rugby, we're moving all over the field with them, so we're knackered by the end of the game just sat in a chair.

We used to go to the allotments, now we end up going

to Asda or Sainsbury's. The baker's has gone, and the butcher and the grocer.

But if you give in, then that's when you are old. You can never give in.

One of the men at the Shed asked the crucial question of 'What makes a man?'

The answers came thick and fast:

'Being able to take it on the chin.'

'Always believing in other people.'

'Admitting you're wrong and listening to others.'

'We can all be friends no matter where we come from.'

'Don't be single-minded and accept other viewpoints.'

'Being a man is being the best version of yourself. After all, what else is there?'

My journey through the Men's Shed has been an inspiration and an eye-opener, but I truly believe if we stick together we will get there... wherever we want to go.